D0031686

Margaret Thatcher

Margaret Thatcher

A Life and Legacy

DAVID CANNADINE

Great Clarendon Street, Oxford, OX2 6DP,
United Kingdom

Oxford University Press is a department of the University of Oxford.
It furthers the University's objective of excellence in research, scholarship,
and education by publishing worldwide. Oxford is a registered trade mark of
Oxford University Press in the UK and in certain other countries

First Edition published in 2017

Impression: 1

Published in the United States of America by Oxford University Press
198 Madison Avenue, New York, NY 10016, United States of America

British Library Cataloguing in Publication Data
Data available

Library of Congress Control Number: 2016957142

ISBN 978–0–19–879500–1

Printed and bound in Italy by
Lego

In memory of
Mrs Thurman

'The full accounting of how my political work affected the lives of others is something we will only know on Judgment Day.'

(Margaret Thatcher, 1995)[1]

TABLE OF CONTENTS

PREFACE

I first encountered what was in retrospect Margaret Thatcher's avatar and anticipation during the autumn of 1955, when I began my formal education as a pupil at a state-funded, Church of England primary school on the western side of Birmingham. The school's headmistress was 'Mrs Thurman' (or 'Mrs T'), and she was a figure by turns unforgettable, intimidating, charismatic, and inspirational. She was always impeccably coiffured, she often wore well-cut blue suits, she was tirelessly and overwhelmingly energetic, and when she lost her temper she was utterly terrifying, reducing not only her errant pupils, but also grown men, to quivering jelly and tearful wrecks. She was a brilliant headmistress. Her motto for her school was 'Only the best is good enough', and she constantly urged us all to strive to make the most that we could of ourselves. It was not until later life that I came to realize just how much I owed her. Unlike many in the teaching profession of her day, Mrs Thurman was a staunch Conservative; she was also a committed Christian, and a vehement anti-Communist, and I can still recall the speech she gave, at a morning assembly in 1956, denouncing the Soviet invasion of Hungary as an unconscionable act of tyranny and aggression.

So when Margaret Thatcher burst upon the British political scene during the 1970s, initially as Secretary of State for Education, and subsequently as Conservative Party leader and Prime Minister, I thought that I already knew something about this second 'Mrs T': for in her appearance, energy, demeanour, and attitudes she seemed to bear a close resemblance to Mrs Thurman, albeit multiplied by a hundred. For most of the 1980s, I lived and worked in Britain, and, like many people, I regarded Thatcher as in some ways admirable, but in others difficult to take. From 1988 to 1998, I taught British history at Columbia University in New York: Thatcher was a marvellous subject on which to lecture, she invested Britain and thus British history with renewed interest and fascination for a transatlantic audience, and she was warmly and widely admired by American Republicans, who could not understand why her own party had turned against her in November 1990. On returning to work in the United Kingdom, I found myself sitting on a University of London committee that Margaret Thatcher chaired, and the early impressions that I had formed of her were amply confirmed. She was past her prime-ministerial prime, but it did not require much imagination to recognize and appreciate how impressive she must have been at the peak of her powers, both in terms of the extraordinary force of her intimidating personality and her complete mastery of the business in hand.

By the time Thatcher died in 2013 she had been in public life for more than forty years, she had been the dominant figure in Britain during the 1980s, I had seen how she had been regarded on both sides of the Atlantic, and thanks to my earlier encounters with Mrs Thurman I had, albeit inadvertently, been given more than just an inkling of the remarkable person that she undoubtedly was. So when, two years ago, my colleagues at the *Oxford Dictionary of National Biography* urged that I should contribute the entry on her, I found the invitation – and the challenge – irresistible. It would be the largest entry for any twentieth-century prime minister since Churchill's, but with the added complication that while some people regarded her, like him, as having been the saviour of her country, others saw her in a completely different light. 'Divisive' was the word often used to describe Thatcher, by friend and foe alike, during her decade of power and on into her retirement, and it continues to be applied in the years since her death. In writing my entry on her, I sought to be as even-handed as possible, viewing her with what I regard as a necessary and deserving combination of sympathy (she was a major historical figure, with many admirable qualities) and detachment (her critics, both inside the Conservative Party and far beyond, often had a case, although not invariably so).

While I was working on my *ODNB* entry, Oxford University Press also decided to publish it as a separate, stand-alone volume. Although my essay on Thatcher is one of the largest in the *Dictionary*, it makes for a relatively concise book when put between hard covers. As many authors have observed, from Pascal onwards, writing short carries with it as many challenges as writing long, and having produced histories and biographies not only at length but also more briefly,

I am well aware of just how different those challenges are. And while history and biography are often regarded as close and kindred activities, anyone who has tried their hand at both genres also knows that in some ways the approaches and sensibilities they require are far from being the same. In the pages that follow, I have tried to give fitting attention to each stage of Thatcher's remarkable career, and to do as much justice as the constraints of space allowed to the many issues by which she was preoccupied in her public life. I have also sought to set her biography in a broader historical context, and to view her prime ministership from the longer-term perspective that is now available, more than a quarter of a century since she ceased to hold the office. As such, this slim volume makes no claim to anticipate or provide the 'full accounting' of Judgment Day to which Thatcher attached such importance, but it does offer what I hope is a readable and reliable version of her life for our times.

In writing the original *ODNB* entry, and in preparing it for publication as a book, my first thanks go to my colleagues at the *Dictionary*, Philip Carter, Mark Curthoys and (especially) Alex May, and to Jo Payne of Oxford University Press, not only for persuading me to take on this task, but also for their sustained help, constant engagement, and encouraging support while I was discharging and completing it. Three exemplary Britons, namely Charles Moore, Stuart Proffitt, and Peter Riddell, made detailed and penetrating comments on my earlier drafts, correcting errors of fact, and greatly improving my final text. Four good American friends, Gary MacDowell, Emerson S. Moore, and Dan and Michelle

Waterman, constantly reminded me of the importance of the transatlantic dimension and perspective. Linda Colley and I lived through most of the 1980s together, and much that I have written here has been influenced by her views and informed by her recollections. And from the beginning to the end of this enterprise, the daunting and demanding shade of Mrs Thurman has never been far away. I dare to hope that she would have approved of the result, and that she might even have recognized some reflections of herself in the pages that follow.

David Cannadine

Princeton
13 October 2016

1

Bound for Politics, 1925–59

'I did not grow up with the sense of division and conflict between classes.'

(Margaret Thatcher, 1995)[1]

'[Margaret] always stood out because teenage girls don't know where they're going. She did.'

(Shirley Ellis, a childhood friend)[2]

Grantham to Oxford

Margaret Hilda Roberts was born at 1 North Parade, Grantham, Lincolnshire, on 13 October 1925, the younger daughter of Alfred Roberts and his wife, Beatrice Ethel, *née* Stephenson. Although she distanced herself from her hometown at the earliest opportunity, and seldom felt nostalgic towards it in her years of power and fame, Grantham was very important in the life and mental make-up of the woman who achieved national renown and international celebrity as 'Mrs Thatcher'. Situated at the north-eastern extremity of the English midlands,

Grantham was a provincial market town, on the main road (A1) and the east coast railway line (LNER) from London to Edinburgh, with a population holding steady at about 20,000 throughout the inter-war years. There was little by way of heavy industry or a factory-based working class, and its civic politics were largely consensual and non-partisan—except, as Thatcher remembered and regretted, in the case of the Labour Party. The local grandees were the Brownlows, who lived nearby at Belton House, and the fifth Baron Brownlow was serving as mayor of Grantham in 1925, the year of Margaret's birth. There was no large-scale unemployment of the kind that was found in the manufacturing towns and cities of the north, but Grantham shared the hardships of the late 1920s and early 1930s, and in the economic recovery that came later in the years immediately before the Second World War. Despite the excellent rail and road connections north and south, the great cities of London and Edinburgh were far away, not only geographically, but culturally and socially as well.

Inter-war Grantham was a somewhat claustrophobic pool, where Alfred Roberts was becoming a big fish when his second daughter (he and Beatrice had no more children) was born. His father had been a Northamptonshire bootmaker, from whom he may have inherited his unostentatious Liberal politics; and in his sustained determination to improve himself, and to be of service to his fellow citizens, Margaret's father might have stepped straight from the pages of Samuel Smiles's *Self-Help*, a book which later became talismanic to his younger daughter. He had left school at thirteen because, being one of a large family, he needed to earn his living, and he went into the grocery trade. But he was also eager to make his way in the world, and this he did by voracious reading, and by his active involvement in the Methodist church. By the time he moved to Grantham and married Beatrice Stephenson, he had saved enough money to acquire a shop on North Parade, and not long before Margaret was born he opened a second store on Huntingtower Road. From this base Alfred Roberts launched himself into the civic life of the town: he was a lay preacher at the Methodist chapel; he became a Rotarian and a justice of the peace; he was a local councillor, elected as an Independent; he was a governor of Kesteven and Grantham Girls' School; and he would later become an alderman and serve as mayor of Grantham in 1945–6.

Margaret Roberts was born above the family shop, and her upbringing was spartan: there was no garden, the lavatory was outside, and there was no hot water. Her parents were not rich, although the family business would prosper in a modest sort of way. But Alfred Roberts loathed any form of extravagance and hated anything that smacked of self-indulgence. The domestic regime over which he presided was austere and puritanical, joyless, and lacking in warmth. At least twice every Sunday, Margaret and her sister, Muriel, were taken to worship at the Finkin Street Methodist Church, where their father often preached the sermon. From an early age the girls were taught the importance of order, precision, and attention to detail; they were escorted on weekly visits to the local library to borrow improving books; as soon as they were old enough, they served behind the counter in the family shop; conversation at home was earnest and high-minded; and Alfred and Beatrice rarely took holidays. Thrift, hard work, self-help, self-reliance, and self-improvement were the governing imperatives of the Roberts household; duty invariably came before pleasure, and public service before personal gratification. Integrity mattered above all else, and it was important to hold opinions because they were right, not because they were popular.

These were the lessons learned, and the virtues internalized, by the young Margaret Roberts, and as prime minister she would later celebrate them as the 'Victorian values' which she believed had made the United Kingdom great in the past, and which under her leadership would make it great again. 'We were Methodists', she would recall, invoking one aspect of her father's legacy, 'and Methodist means method'.[3] 'Those poor shopkeepers!', she allegedly exclaimed in the summer of 1981, invoking another, on hearing of the damaged retail stores in the Toxteth riots.[4] When prime minister, Thatcher would declare that she owed 'almost everything' to her father.[5] Her relations with her mother were never as close. Yet Margaret learned more from Beatrice than she would later admit, for although she would never be a conventional housewife, she liked to clean, to sew, and to decorate and furnish the places where she lived; she would often provide late-night meals for her personal staff at 10 Downing Street; and she would elevate the domestic verities of hearth and home into governing principles and political imperatives. 'Some say I preach merely the homilies of housekeeping or the parables of the parlour', she told the lord mayor's banquet in November 1982. 'But I do not repent. Those parables would have saved many a financier from failure and many a country from crisis'.[6]

Alfred Roberts was self-made and self-taught, but he was determined that his daughters should be given every educational opportunity he had been denied. Both girls attended the local primary school, and later went on to Kesteven and Grantham Girls' School, of whose governors Roberts would eventually become chairman. Margaret won a scholarship, she was serious, intelligent, competitive, and hard-working, possessed great powers of concentration, and was already hyperactive and seemed able to get by with very little sleep. She kept her distance from the other girls, and in later life would prefer the company of men to that of women; but she also played hockey for the school team, liked dancing and going to the cinema, and evinced an early interest in elegant and stylish clothes. She also took elocution classes, won prizes for recitations, and became a confident and well-prepared debater. She sat her school certificate in the summer of 1941, and obtained distinctions in chemistry, arithmetic, and algebra. In the sixth form she specialized in the sciences, particularly chemistry, because she believed they were 'the way of the future' (and she may have been influenced by the fact that Grantham's most famous son was Sir Isaac Newton). She also evinced a growing fascination with the law, from seeing her father in action at the magistrates' court.

Margaret Roberts was brighter, more energetic, and more ambitious than her sister, Muriel (who was training in Birmingham to be a physiotherapist), and with the encouragement of her father she set her sights on gaining a scholarship to Oxford University (the money would be essential). She sat the exam for Somerville College in the autumn of 1942, but narrowly failed to win an award; instead she was offered an ordinary place for the autumn of 1944, and resigned herself to filling in with an extra year at school, of which she now became joint head girl. But someone who had taken a place at Somerville for the autumn of 1943 unexpectedly dropped out; it was offered to Margaret Roberts and she accepted, her father being determined to pay the bills somehow. 'Margaret', her final school report concluded, 'is ambitious and deserves to do well'.[7] She would become a lifelong admirer of grammar schools, which she regarded as providing a ladder of opportunity for people from unprivileged backgrounds, and when she accepted a peerage in 1992 she took her territorial designation from her school, not from her home town. Yet this would not prevent her, as secretary of state for education between 1970 and 1974, from acquiescing, albeit reluctantly, in the closure of more grammar schools than anyone in her position has done, before or since.

The road to Westminster

Oxford would eventually provide the route whereby Margaret Roberts escaped the cloying limitations of English provincial life. But the ancient university town was far from Grantham in more ways than one, and when she first appeared at Somerville, she had spent scarcely a night away from home. She was initially apprehensive, homesick, and lonely, and having failed to win a scholarship, was almost always short of money. Then, as later, her response to adversity was to work harder than ever, and harder than anyone else. As at school, she was an able and highly motivated student, but neither of the academics with whom she came into the closest contact considered her brilliant. Janet Vaughan, who became principal of Somerville in 1945, thought her 'a perfectly good second-class chemist';[8] while Dorothy Hodgkin, the future Nobel laureate and probably the most eminent woman with whom Margaret ever dealt (both would become members of the Order of Merit), rated her as 'good. One could always rely on her producing a sensible, well-read essay'.[9] Hodgkin employed her as a research assistant during her fourth year, and Margaret duly obtained a sound second-class degree. For the rest of her life she retained a genuine interest in the sciences. She would later claim that being the first prime minister to have graduated in one of those subjects was a more signal achievement than being the first woman to occupy 10 Downing Street, and the speech she delivered to the Royal Society in 1988 expressing concern about global warming would be the first by a major world leader.

Somerville tended to be left-wing in its political sympathies, and that was certainly true of Vaughan and Hodgkin. But Margaret Roberts had already espoused a very different creed, and once again her father was the formative figure. By the mid-1930s Alfred Roberts had become a Conservative in all but name: he disliked the Co-operative Party, which controlled Labour in Grantham and was opposed to independent shopkeepers like himself. At the general election of 1935 he signed the nomination papers of the local Tory candidate, Sir Victor Warrender, and at the time of Munich he was an ardent supporter of Neville Chamberlain and his policy of appeasement. Margaret Roberts absorbed most (but not all) of her father's views, and her first direct involvement in politics was working for Warrender on polling day. At Somerville she joined the Oxford University Conservative Association and in her final year became its president, the highest political office to which a woman undergraduate could then aspire, since membership of the Oxford Union was restricted to men. She met such leading Tories as Peter Thorneycroft (whom she made party chairman in 1975); she campaigned in the general election of 1945 for Quintin Hogg (who as Lord Hailsham she would appoint as her lord chancellor in 1979); she reorganized the University Conservative Association and increased membership; and, as a young 'representative', she began to attend national gatherings of the party faithful.

By the time she left Oxford in the summer of 1947 Margaret Roberts was a very different person from the anxious and lonely figure who had arrived at Somerville four years earlier. She would never fully conquer the insecurities deriving from her lowly born status, but she was already set on a political career, and her views were conventionally Conservative: strong admiration for Winston Churchill, a firm belief in the greatness of Britain and its empire, support for the ideas of John Maynard Keynes and William Beveridge on employment and social security, and dismay at the outcome of the general election of 1945 (and she read F. A. Hayek's *Road to Serfdom*, which attacked the idea of an ever more intrusive state and reasserted the importance of free-market freedom, although it made little impact on her at the time). But Oxford had not been all work and politics, as she had discovered a broader and richer life than Grantham had offered. For the University Conservative Association was a social as well as a political organization, and despite being constantly short of money, Margaret Roberts enjoyed the dinners and the dances, and she always dressed well, borrowing clothes and jewellery from her sister. Oxford also provided her first boyfriends, and she took one of them, Tony Bray, to Grantham, where he attended chapel with her parents. But, by then, Margaret was distancing herself from her family and her home-town, and although she remained loyal to her father's values and example her professional, political, and personal lives would all be spent in London and the south-east.

After graduation Margaret Roberts found work as a research chemist, initially with British Xylonite Plastics, located at Manningtree in Essex (which produced the materials for spectacle frames), and then with J. Lyons & Co. at Hammersmith in London (where she tested the quality of cake fillings and ice cream). But while these were her day jobs, her real passion was politics, and thanks to the connections she had made in Oxford, her assiduous attendance at party conferences, and her impressive performance before the selection committee, she was adopted as the prospective parliamentary candidate for the Dartford constituency in Kent. There was no chance that she would win, since it was a safe Labour seat, but in the general elections of February 1950 and October 1951, when she was the youngest Conservative candidate in the contests, she campaigned with energy and determination, attracted considerable media attention, and reduced the Labour majority from 19,714 in 1945 to 13,638 in 1950, and 12,334 the following year. (The seat was to remain in Labour hands until the 1970 election.) She also continued to mix politics and pleasure. One boyfriend was a Scottish farmer, Willie Cullen, who would later marry her sister, Muriel; another was a doctor, Robert Henderson, who was twice her age. On the evening of her adoption meeting for Dartford she met a man who was 'very reserved but quite nice', with 'plenty of money', and who was 'a perfect gentleman'.[10] His name was Denis Thatcher, and he and Margaret were married on 13 December 1951.

Like several of the men with whom she had gone out, Denis Thatcher was considerably older than the woman who would one day make his name world famous. He had attended a public school, and had served as a staff officer in the army during the Second World War, when he was mentioned in dispatches. He was active in the Dartford Conservative Association, but he had no political ambitions for himself. By the time he met Margaret Roberts he was the manager of a prosperous family business, which made paints, wood preservers, deck cleaners, and industrial chemicals, and for which he had worked, apart from the war years, since 1934. He had married Margaret Kempson in 1942, but by the time he was demobilized in 1946 she had left him for another man, and they divorced soon after. Denis was determined to remarry, but his careful courtship of Margaret Roberts lasted well over two years. Nor was she initially smitten with him, as she had been with Robert Henderson. But Denis was an ex-soldier, he was athletic and well-dressed, he knew about business and money, he had a certain 'style and dash',[11] and he drove a Jaguar. Although Margaret was the better educated of the two, Denis was much richer, and offered a passport to the home counties identity and respectability she was determined to acquire.

Her marriage transformed the second Margaret Thatcher's life, beginning with their honeymoon in Madeira, which was the first time she had been abroad, and she soon completed the task of distancing herself from her home, her family, her class, and her religion (Margaret and Denis married at Wesley's Chapel in London's City Road, but thereafter moved towards the Church of England, and in her last years she was a regular worshipper at the Royal Hospital, Chelsea). Denis reinforced many of her political views, especially her dislike of the Labour Party and trades unions, and her support for the British empire in general and for white South Africa in particular. He also brought her the financial security she had not previously known, and she would never have to work for a living. But being a full-time housewife held no allure, and she decided to read for the bar, enrolling at the Inns of Court School of Law in early 1952. She passed her exams in December 1953, was called to the bar by Lincoln's Inn soon after, and specialized in the subject of tax law. The experience of mastering complex financial arguments would stand her in good stead in later life, and she came to believe that the rule of law was an essential aspect of freedom and democracy. In August 1953 she had given birth to twins: Carol and Mark. Margaret and Denis were genuinely fond of their children, but he was often abroad on business, and she was determined that they would neither interfere with her legal activities nor thwart her political ambitions. The Thatchers could afford ample childcare, and Carol and Mark were sent away to school at the earliest opportunity.

Thatcher had made her position plain on such matters in an article in the *Sunday Graphic* published in February 1952. Women, she believed, should not feel obliged to stay at home: they should embrace careers, thereby developing talents and abilities that would otherwise be wasted. More of them should go into politics, and if they were good enough, they ought to rise to high office: perhaps to be chancellor of the exchequer or foreign secretary (but that was as far as she was willing to speculate). Later that year an event occurred which Thatcher never forgot or forgave, and which further turned her against her home town and also against Labour-controlled local authorities. After thirty years of public service Alderman Alfred Roberts was brutally thrown off the Grantham town council by the controlling Labour group, in an act which his daughter regarded as mean-spirited, vindictive, and ungrateful. The following month, in June 1952, she renewed her search for a constituency, and she applied unsuccessfully for several seats in the south-east. But her persistence paid off, and in March 1958 she was shortlisted for the safe Conservative seat of Finchley, a moderately prosperous, *petit bourgeois*, owner-occupied London suburb, with a significant Jewish population. She was adopted, and at the general election of October 1959 she increased the previous majority of 12,825 to 16,260. From this secure and impregnable base, she would launch and sustain the most extraordinary political career of modern times.

2

Unexpected Leader, 1959–79

> 'I think it would be extremely difficult for a woman to make it to the top.'
>
> (Margaret Thatcher, 1974)[1]

> 'I doubt that most of the Tory MPs who had voted for Thatcher at the time understood quite what they had done; perhaps she did not understand it herself.'
>
> (William Waldegrave, 2015)[2]

MP to secretary of state

Margaret Thatcher was one of only twelve women Conservative MPs among the Commons intake of 1959, but unlike the rest of them she hit the ground running. By good fortune she immediately came second in the annual ballot for parliamentary time to sponsor a private member's bill, which meant she introduced her first piece of legislation in her maiden speech on 5 February 1960. The aim of the measure was to prevent local councils from excluding the press from their meetings, as some of them, usually Labour-controlled, had recently been doing. It was an early example of Thatcher's abiding hostility to organized labour and trade union power, and her speech introducing the bill was widely praised for its command of detail, and for the fluency and conviction with which she delivered it. In October 1961 the prime minister, Harold Macmillan, appointed her parliamentary secretary to the minister of pensions, the lowliest rung on the government ladder, and a post usually given to a woman, because pensions, like education, were deemed a 'feminine' subject. Thatcher rapidly mastered the complexities of such arcane issues as national insurance, and on the whole took a favourable view of her officials; indeed the permanent secretary, Sir Eric Bowyer, rather admired her.

For three years Thatcher continued her work at the Ministry of Pensions. Despite some qualms that public spending was increasing too much, she generally went along with government policies, including the decision to apply to join the Common Market. She thought Macmillan was losing his grip by the end of his premiership, and she became a strong supporter of the fourteenth earl of Home as his successor in October 1963. At the general election of October 1964, which Labour won by the slimmest of margins, she easily held Finchley, but with her majority reduced to 8,802. Soon after, Denis suffered a nervous breakdown, and for a time the Thatchers' marriage seemed in jeopardy. The management of the family company was becoming increasingly burdensome; he had a mother, a sister, and an aunt to look after; and Margaret's hyper-energy and almost complete absorption in politics left him exhausted, lonely, and confused. Later in 1964 Denis sailed to South Africa, where he stayed for two months: neither he nor Margaret knew whether he would return to her. It was the greatest crisis of their marriage; but Denis came back, and soon afterwards he sold the family company to Castrol on very advantageous terms, and they immediately re-employed him. Castrol was later taken over by Burmah Oil, of which Denis became a director, and he eventually retired in 1975, the same year that Margaret would win the Conservative Party leadership.

From 1964 to 1970 the Tories were in opposition, and Sir Alec Douglas-Home (as the earl of Home had become on disclaiming his peerage) resigned as party leader in July 1965. The effective choice as his successor was between Reginald Maudling and Edward Heath, and Thatcher voted for Heath because she thought he would be better at taking on the Labour leader, Harold Wilson. During her years in opposition she held six shadow posts. She was a junior spokesman for pensions, then housing and land (from October 1965), then Treasury affairs (after the general election of March 1966, when she bucked the national trend by increasing her majority to 9464); on being promoted to the shadow cabinet in October 1967 she was successively responsible for fuel and power, transport (from November 1968), and finally education (from October 1969). She mastered these many different briefs with varying enthusiasm, but she engaged with all of them with unfailing energy, application, and efficiency. Her combative Commons performances consistently impressed by her command of detail and her fearless determination to take on some of Labour's biggest names over such controversial issues as the imposition of selective employment tax. But the chemistry between Thatcher and Heath did not work, as her undeniable assertiveness grated with his incorrigible abrasiveness, and he promoted her only belatedly and grudgingly to the shadow cabinet, fearing—rightly, as it turned out—that 'we'll never be able to get rid of her'.[3]

Being in opposition also gave Thatcher the freedom to undertake extensive foreign travel for the first time: not for self-indulgent holidays, but for serious and self-improving purposes. She visited Israel, Sweden, and the Soviet Union, but she paid little heed to the heartlands of Europe, and her two longest and most important trips were to the United States, in 1967 and 1969. Official Washington did not consider her sufficiently significant to put itself out for her, but she travelled widely across the country, and found America exciting and enthralling. She liked the welcoming warmth of its people; she admired their entrepreneurial energy, their belief in the free market, and their determined and simultaneous pursuit of wealth and self-improvement; and she thought Britain might learn from the example of a governing and fiscal regime that was less intrusive in its reach and less punitive in its taxation. These were scarcely original or nuanced views of a vast and varied country; but to Thatcher, America's values and aspirations bore a striking resemblance to those she had learned at her father's knee, and the United States would become the model for what she wanted to achieve in Britain. Yet while America offered international validation for the corner-shop culture with which she had grown up in Grantham, her ties to her home town and family further attenuated as her own horizons widened. Alfred Roberts saw little of his daughter in his later years, and he died in February 1970, a few months before she entered the cabinet.

When the Conservatives won the general election held in June 1970, Thatcher was the obvious choice to be Heath's secretary of state for education: she had held the shadow portfolio, and since it was thought necessary to have at least one woman in the cabinet she had the most commanding claim. She was not a transformative departmental minister: she had no developed philosophy of education, beyond an abiding loyalty to grammar schools and a belief in the importance of élite universities, and she neither initiated any major reforms nor carried any significant legislation. She was impressive but not visionary, mastering the business, combative in the Commons, and successfully fending off the persistent Treasury demands that expenditure be reined in. Indeed, Thatcher wanted more money for her department, not less, as was set out in the policy document *Education: a Framework for Expansion* (Cmnd 5174), published in December 1972, which advocated and predicted a massive rise in government spending on education over the next decade. Her determination and energy earned her the respect of her civil servants, but not their affection. Unlike at pensions, she did not think much of them. She thought the ethos of the department was 'self-righteously socialist',[4] and she regarded the permanent secretary, Sir William Pile, as condescending and disloyal, and she vainly sought to get him replaced.

Thatcher's first decision as secretary of state was to cancel Circular 10/65, by which the previous Labour government had tried to force local authorities to embrace comprehensive schooling. But the tide was running so strongly in that direction that both Labour- and Conservative-controlled councils continued to submit comprehensive schemes, and she had little power to resist them. She rejected only 326 of the 3,612 proposals she received, and the proportion of pupils in England and Wales attending comprehensives rose from 32 to 62 per cent during her tenure. She also continued the policies of the Labour government by saving the Open University, which Harold Wilson had established in 1969: many of her cabinet colleagues wanted it closed down, but she believed it extended educational opportunity. Within a year of taking office Thatcher became embroiled in her first public controversy, when she sought to abolish free milk for schoolchildren between the ages of seven and eleven, so as to make some short-term savings. The proposal aroused a storm of protest from the Labour opposition and the popular press; she was denounced as 'Mrs Thatcher, the milk-snatcher', and declared to be 'The Most Unpopular Woman in Britain'.[5] The attacks hit her hard; she briefly thought of leaving politics altogether, and Heath considered sacking her. It later transpired that her civil servants had failed to warn her of the likely public fallout. This was the first time, but not the last, that she was let down by poor staff work.

The 'milk-snatcher' fiasco seemed to vindicate Heath's view that education would be the highest office Thatcher would achieve in public life. Despite the importance that was attached to schooling in post-war Britain, the department was widely regarded as a dead-end ministerial post, whether held by a man or a woman. To be sure, it had a large (and growing) budget; but this was primarily spent on buildings and infrastructure. In schools the employment of teachers and the control of the curriculum remained local authority matters; and in higher education the University Grants Committee had been created to keep the government at arm's length. From the outset of her tenure Thatcher regretted these constraints, and after two years, by which time the 'milk-snatcher' affair had largely subsided, she hankered for a more 'mainline' job. But Heath declined to promote her, and education would be the only ministerial portfolio she would hold before she became party leader. Thereafter she kept her head down and avoided controversial subjects, concentrating on expanding nursery education, funding more primary schools, raising the school leaving age from fifteen to sixteen, and establishing more polytechnics. (Despite her close involvement with the state sector Margaret and Denis sent their own children to be educated privately: Carol at St Paul's Girls' School, and Mark at Harrow.)

But while Thatcher was minding her own business at education, Heath's government was running into serious trouble. He had come to power determined to get the United Kingdom into the Common Market, which he duly did, and he was also eager to shrink the state and free up the economy. Yet he soon abandoned these domestic policies. In 1971 the cabinet rescued Rolls-Royce and the upper Clyde shipyards, despite an earlier undertaking never to bail out such 'lame ducks'. Early in the following year the miners went on strike, and Britain was reduced to working a three-day week. They won a 20 per cent pay rise, in response to which Heath imposed a statutory freeze on wages and prices. His attempts to curb growing trade union militancy by legislation were unsuccessful, inflation reached double-digit levels, the outbreak of the Yom Kippur War in the Middle East meant oil prices would almost quadruple between October 1973 and January 1974, and by then the miners were prepared to do battle again. In cabinet Thatcher spoke out against trade union militancy, state support for lame ducks, and the prices and incomes policy; but she gained little traction, and in public she defended this succession of policy U-turns. In February 1974 Heath called a general election, fought on the question 'Who governs Britain?', in which Thatcher played no prominent national part. Her Finchley majority was almost halved, from 11,185 to 5,978, and although the Tories gained a larger share of the national vote, they won four fewer seats than Labour. Heath failed to form a coalition with the Liberals, he resigned on 4 March, and Thatcher again found herself in opposition.

Party leader to prime minister

Wilson formed a minority government; Heath determined to remain Conservative leader, despite mounting back-bench criticism, and he gave Thatcher the environment portfolio in his shadow cabinet. In discussing the manifesto for the next election, which it was widely recognized must come soon, she reluctantly agreed to propose that the mortgage rate (then at an unprecedented 11 per cent) should never go above 9.5 per cent. Yet she was privately unhappy with this policy, which portended further state intervention; and her free-market misgivings were corroborated and encouraged by her friend Sir Keith Joseph and the Centre for Policy Studies (CPS) which he now established, and of which Thatcher became vice-chairman. Urged on by Joseph, the CPS began to adumbrate a new Conservative philosophy, which distanced itself from all Tory administrations since 1951, including Heath's. Nationalization, state intervention, prices and incomes policies, and irresponsible public spending were all denounced as the negation of the true Conservative principles of free enterprise, a minimalist state, and the strict regulation of public spending. Moreover, unemployment was no longer the main threat to prosperity and stability, as it had been during the inter-war years. The great danger was inflation; and the solution was for governments to stop printing more money, as they had done since the late 1950s, and to start printing less.

Encouraged by Joseph, Thatcher began to question the basis of Conservative politics that had prevailed since she had entered public life; she re-read Hayek and devoured more recent works by such writers as Milton Friedman; and she engaged with the free-market ideas being put forward by Ralph Harris and Arthur Seldon at the Institute of Economic Affairs. But in public she kept close to her shadow responsibilities, and barely expressed any dissent from the leadership. When Wilson called another general election for mid-October 1974, Thatcher's specific policy promises (to introduce the right to buy for council house tenants, to keep mortgage rates below 9.5 per cent, and to replace the domestic rates with a fairer system of local taxation) were almost the only ones put forward in the Conservative campaign. But she was less enamoured of the manifesto commitment to a prices and incomes policy, and she was especially annoyed at Heath's call for a government of 'national unity', making it plain that she would not sit round a cabinet table with such left-wing politicians as Michael Foot and Tony Benn. Nor did it seem likely that Heath himself, who had become such a divisive figure, could lead an administration pledged to cross-party consensus. In the end Labour gained an overall Commons majority of three, the Conservatives lost twenty seats, and Thatcher held Finchley by only 3,911 votes. Like many Conservatives she believed that Heath had to go, and she hoped Joseph would succeed him.

But Heath refused to stand down, and there was no formal procedure for challenging, or deposing, an incumbent Tory leader. He grudgingly conceded that the rules should be changed, and following the adoption of recommendations from a review chaired by Douglas-Home an election was scheduled for February 1975, in which only Tory MPs would vote. The first casualty of the jockeying to succeed Heath was Joseph, who in a speech nine days after the general election made some ill-judged remarks about the intellectual and moral shortcomings of those at the lower end of the social scale. There was a press and public outcry, Joseph recognized that he could never win the Conservative leadership, and Thatcher resolved to stand in his stead. None of Heath's former cabinet colleagues was prepared to oppose him, and she began to gather support from backbench MPs who had had enough of his rudeness and failures, and who admired her pluck in standing against him. Thatcher's campaign was expertly organized by the back-bench MP Airey Neave, whereas Heath was merely bad-tempered and resentful, mistakenly believing the leadership would remain his. On the first ballot, held on 4 February, she won 130 votes to Heath's 119. Under the new rules this was an insufficient majority, but Heath immediately resigned, never to hold office again, and his former deputy, Willie Whitelaw, declared himself the candidate of unity and moderation. But Thatcher's bandwagon could not be stopped, and on the second ballot, held on 11 February, she beat Whitelaw by 146 votes to 79. It was a conclusive victory, and at the age of forty-nine, she became the first woman leader of a British political party.

Thatcher had been elected more because she was not Heath, a difference which he gender advantageously emphasized, than because she offered alternative policies. Most Tory MPs did not know what she thought on most issues, or how much her ideas had been evolving in private in recent months. Moreover, her shadow cabinet looked very much like Heath's, with the predictable exception that he was not in it. (Heath never forgave Thatcher for supplanting him, and would be her implacable but increasingly impotent enemy for the rest of his days.) The majority of her senior colleagues had remained his loyal supporters until the end, and only one of them, Joseph, had voted for her. So despite her victory in the leadership election, Thatcher was in a weak position, for while her sex had been an asset in differentiating her from Heath, it proved less of an advantage once she had assumed the party leadership.

Tory grandees such as Lord Carrington, Sir Ian Gilmour, Christopher Soames, and Whitelaw looked down on her, on account of her gender and her lowly social origins, condescensions vividly articulated in Whitelaw's description of her as 'governessy'.[6] It was the same in the Conservative Research Department, presided over by Chris Patten, where Thatcher was referred to as 'Hilda' or 'milk-snatcher'.[7] And many Tory MPs, drawn from the male worlds of public schools, regiments, professions, boardrooms, and clubs, soon began to wonder what they had been doing when they voted for *her*.

During her early months as Conservative leader Thatcher was very much on probation. When Wilson called a referendum on Britain's continued membership of the Common Market, she favoured staying in, but she left most of the campaigning to Heath, which put him back in the limelight, and for a brief time in a positive way. Although Wilson was not the man he had been in the 1960s he was still clever and cunning enough to get the better of Thatcher at prime minister's question time, while his successor from April 1976, James Callaghan, who had already been chancellor of the exchequer, home secretary, and foreign secretary, patronized her unrelentingly for her lack of experience of high office and in international affairs. She could not command the overwhelmingly male-dominated Commons, and nor was she in full control of her own party's policy-making process, as revealed in two papers published by Conservative Central Office, *The Right Approach* (1976) and *The Right Approach to the Economy* (1977). They made a definite commitment to 'the firm management of government expenditure',[8] but there was no comparable undertaking to tackle the trades unions, while returning nationalized industries to the private sector rated scarcely a mention. They were cautious and pragmatic documents rather than ideological and crusading manifestos.

At this point Thatcher did not seem a plausible prime minister in waiting, and nor, in her public views, was she a Thatcherite *avant la lettre*. But as always she was determined to improve and do better. She took advice from Gordon Reece, a former television producer, about her clothes and appearance, and worked with a voice coach at the National Theatre to lower her pitch and soften her tone. She made two speeches denouncing the Soviet Union for being set on world domination, in response to which the Russian media dubbed her the 'Iron Lady'—much to her delight. She travelled widely in Europe, the Middle East, south Asia, and the Far East; she twice returned to the United States, where she was taken more seriously than on previous visits; and in April 1975 she met Ronald Reagan, a former Hollywood actor and governor of California, and by then a presidential hopeful. She hired an advertising agency, run by the brothers Charles and Maurice Saatchi, to handle the party's public relations, and they would coin for her the election-winning slogan 'Labour isn't working'. The Conservatives gradually gained ground in the polls, and Callaghan made a fatal error in not calling an election in the autumn of 1978, preferring to wait until the following spring. But the months in between became known as the 'winter of discontent', as a succession of destructive strikes by workers in the private and public sectors, demanding inflationary wage claims, meant that for weeks refuse went uncollected, graves went undug, ambulances did not turn out, and petrol stations closed.

By then Callaghan seemed no more in control of events than Heath had been five years before. Once again the government's survival was threatened by militant industrial action and by the soaring pay claims of the trades unions, and these spelled the end of Labour's attempts to establish a voluntary incomes policy with their co-operation. Prices and wages were rising, and inflation was increasing; but so, too, was unemployment. This was a new and ominous phenomenon, to which the name 'stagflation' was applied, and it presented an unprecedented challenge to conventional Keynesian economics, according to which stagnation (when unemployment rose) and inflation (when prices rose) were not supposed to co-exist. As Callaghan reluctantly recognized, this meant it was no longer possible for the government to spend its way out of recession, because pumping more money into the economy would merely drive up prices still further. Instead, and as Joseph and the CPS had already recognized, Callaghan and his chancellor, Denis Healey, concluded that the only option left was to try to bring down inflation by restricting the money supply. But although this major change in government policy had been embraced before the Tories regained office and would claim it as their own, it would not save the visibly disintegrating Labour administration. On 30 March 1979 Thatcher carried a no-confidence motion by 311 votes to 310, Callaghan announced that he would be seeking an early election, and parliament was dissolved.

At the beginning of the ensuing campaign the Conservatives were fourteen points ahead of Labour in the polls, although Thatcher's personal rating lagged behind Callaghan's until election day itself. The Tory manifesto contained few specific commitments: business and free enterprise would be encouraged, income tax cut, public borrowing reduced, and the money supply more strictly controlled. But there was no outright opposition to an incomes policy, the trades unions were not targeted for significant reform, and there was scarcely any mention of the privatization of nationalized industry. Thatcher fought a vigorous and energetic campaign, in which she denounced the government's dismal record, and declared that Labour was no longer competent to rule. She also played the patriotic card, lamenting that a once great country had been brought so low, and expressing her firm conviction that national decline could be reversed and Britain's greatness restored. Callaghan retorted that voting for the Tories, and for their untried leader, was too big a gamble. But the electorate disregarded his warning and returned the Conservatives with an overall majority of forty-three; Thatcher herself more than doubled her own majority in Finchley, to 7,878. On 4 May 1979 she became prime minister, confounding her own earlier predictions as to what any woman might achieve in British politics during her lifetime. From the steps of 10 Downing Street she promised, in words erroneously attributed to St Francis of Assisi, to replace discord with harmony, error with truth, doubt with faith, and despair with hope.

3

Challenging Beginnings, 1979–81

'I do not greatly care what people say about me . . . This is the road I am resolved to follow. This is the path I must go.'

(Margaret Thatcher, 1981)[1]

'There is no basis in economic theory or supporting evidence for the Government's belief that by deflating demand, they will bring inflation permanently under control, and thereby introduce an automatic recovery in output and employment.'

(364 economists, letter to *The Times*, 30 March 1981)

Domestic travails

The Thatchers moved into the small flat atop their official residence: as in Grantham, Margaret was again living over the shop. Yet, despite her confident manner and determined public demeanour, she was genuinely unsure of herself now that she had obtained the supreme office. She had never held a senior post in government, her ideas as to what she would do were not thought through, and many in the media and the corridors of power regarded her as a jarring and untried extremist who would not last. Moreover, and like Churchill in 1940 (a comparison she would have relished), Thatcher was far from being in command of her cabinet. She kept Heath out, and he scornfully rejected her strange offer of the Washington embassy. Whitelaw had pledged his support as soon as Thatcher became Tory leader; she made him home secretary and *de facto* deputy prime minister, and he never let her down. She also gave her two closest allies senior posts: Geoffrey Howe was made chancellor of the exchequer, and Joseph became secretary of state for industry. But most of her appointments were of Heathite, 'One Nation' Tories: Carrington at the Foreign Office, Francis Pym at defence, Michael Heseltine at environment, Peter Walker at agriculture, Jim Prior at employment, Gilmour as lord privy seal, Soames as lord president, and Hailsham as lord chancellor.

This was scarcely a government of like-minded colleagues, and Thatcher only got her way on controversial matters of economic policy by ensuring they were never openly discussed in the full cabinet during her first year in office. She faced similar challenges in bending the machinery of government to her will: at education she had formed a low opinion of civil servants, whom she regarded as more concerned with thwarting change than with helping ministers to implement it. But she was able to counter this Whitehall inertia by her sheer energy and force of personality: she read all the papers she was sent, and often returned them covered with critical comments; and she made unannounced visits to the outposts of Whitehall to find out what was going on. Not since Churchill had an incoming prime minister kicked the civil service so hard and worked it so unrelentingly. Yet despite her generally hostile attitude to the men in Whitehall, Thatcher also came to appreciate, and to depend on, the skills and support provided by her two long-serving cabinet secretaries, successively Sir Robert Armstrong (1979–87) and Sir Robin Butler (1988–90). She also appointed a loyal and bluff Yorkshireman, Bernard Ingham, as her press secretary, and Ian Gow as her devoted parliamentary private secretary; between them they kept her in close touch with the media and back-bench Tory opinion.

Although Thatcher had been elected on the promise of making a definite break with the failures of the Wilson, Heath, and Callaghan administrations, there were many indications, during the early years of her government, that little had changed for the better. By the end of 1979 inflation was forecast to reach an even higher level, and business confidence had collapsed since the election. By the summer of 1980 prices had risen 22 per cent in only a single year, and wages by almost as much. By the spring of 1981 gross domestic product was down 5.5 per cent in two years, and unemployment stood at 2.7 million, an increase of one million in the previous twelve months. There were strikes in the steel industry ending with a 16 per cent pay award, and by civil servants, which meant the payment of pensions and family allowances, and the collection of income tax, were for a time in jeopardy. Faced with the threat of further industrial action by the miners and their allies, Thatcher overruled the National Coal Board's plan to close twenty-three uneconomic pits and lose 13,000 jobs: it was a humiliating about-face. Despite his free-market convictions Joseph agreed to bail out the ailing car-manufacturing conglomerate, British Leyland, at a cost that would eventually be in excess of £1 billion, and while Prior's Employment Act of 1980 made it more difficult for trades unions to introduce the closed shop, and outlawed secondary picketing, it did little to curb labour militancy.

Nevertheless, Thatcher and Howe were determined to signal that they were going to change course decisively, even though it had been during the final months of the Callaghan government that inflation had been identified as the great enemy, and the restricting of public spending proposed as the remedy. For they were also hostile to high taxes, and were determined to subject the British economy to the much-needed and bracing discipline of the free market. In his first budget, delivered in June 1979, Howe cut the standard rate of income tax from 33 to 30 per cent, and the top rate from 83 to 60 per cent; public spending was reduced by 3 per cent; and to balance the books, value added tax was almost doubled, from 8 to 15 per cent. This significant break with the recent past was justified on the grounds that since every other remedy had been tried and failed, there was 'no alternative'. In October 1979 Howe announced the complete lifting of exchange controls, which meant that in future the value of sterling would be determined by the foreign exchange markets, and the government would no longer step in to defend the pound. The following month, in a further effort to rein in the money supply, interest rates were raised from 14 to 17 per cent, the highest level ever; and in the budget he presented in March 1980 Howe reiterated the government's commitment to reducing public spending and announced further cuts.

Yet in the short run these policies intensified the very economic ills it was claimed they would cure. Raising value added tax and interest rates fuelled inflation, and provoked renewed calls for increased wage settlements, while it also weakened consumer demand. At the same time the free-floating pound initially rose in value on the foreign exchange markets, because of high interest rates, which made British exports less competitive, and further damaged industrial output. Unemployment kept rising, and the economy continued to contract, but Thatcher was adamant that, unlike Heath, she would not change course. As she told the Tory party conference in October 1980: 'You turn if you want to. The lady's not for turning'.[2] The next March, Howe presented his third budget, which cut spending and increased taxes when the economy was still in its downward spiral. Government borrowing would be reduced by £3.5 billion; a one-off windfall tax was announced on certain bank deposits; the personal allowance on income tax was not increased; and duties on petrol, cigarettes, and alcohol were raised. The only consolation was that interest rates, already lowered from their earlier record level, were further reduced to 12 per cent. But Howe conceded that unemployment would rise to three million; his budget was not well received; and 364 economists wrote to *The Times* warning that 'present policies will deepen the depression, erode the industrial base of our economy, and threaten its social and political stability'.[3]

During her first years in office Thatcher was preoccupied with trying to get the economy right, but there were two other areas of domestic policy in which she was also closely involved. The first, which would be of lasting significance, concerned the sale of council houses. The dream of 'a property-owning democracy' had long been a Tory nostrum, and Thatcher sympathized with the aspirations of those who lived in local authority accommodation but who wished to purchase their homes. The Housing Act of 1980, steered through parliament by Heseltine, gave five million council house tenants 'the right to buy', and at the end of the first Thatcher administration nearly half a million families had availed themselves of its provisions. Her second additional domestic concern was Northern Ireland—a subject on which she had no thought-out policy, beyond a kind of instinctive unionism. She was determined never to yield to Irish nationalist terrorism (the more so after Airey Neave had been assassinated in March 1979, just before she became prime minister), but she also recognized that Dublin and Washington had serious interests in this issue. She faced down the first round of hunger strikes by IRA prisoners (who were demanding 'political' status) in December 1980, and in the same month she led a British delegation to Dublin to meet with Charles Haughey, the taoiseach. The meeting was inconclusive, and it was scarcely coincidence that by then Thatcher, beset by domestic travails, was increasingly involving herself in foreign policy matters.

International initiations

When she became prime minister Thatcher had no first-hand experience of high-level diplomacy. She wanted to make Britain great again, not only domestically but internationally too; but she had little idea of how to go about doing so. As a committed cold war warrior she had delivered some powerful speeches, denouncing communism and the Soviet Union, and she was an ardent admirer of the United States. Although she had supported British entry she was less enamoured of the Common Market than Heath, and she would not warm to President Valéry Giscard d'Estaing of France. She had little time for the Commonwealth, and least of all for its African leaders, who disliked her sympathy for white South Africans, and she was unimpressed by the United Nations, which she scorned as no more than a talking shop. She also regarded the Foreign Office mandarins as incorrigible appeasers who were insufficiently attentive to defending the national interest. But it was a sign of her lack of sure-footedness that she had appointed Carrington to be her foreign secretary, for he was an authentic grandee, with liberal values and paternalistic instincts, and he had been a close ally and supporter of Heath (as had Gilmour who, as lord privy seal, represented the Foreign Office in the Commons). But Carrington was also well travelled, the chemistry with Thatcher worked, and he was the only member of her cabinet who could tease her and get away with it.

From the outset Carrington sought to guide and educate Thatcher in the subtleties and complexities of international affairs, and to rein in her more belligerent views and confrontational instincts. He did not always succeed, but in the case of Rhodesia, which was the United Kingdom's last remaining imperial entanglement in Africa, he soon did. Since 1965, when Ian Smith, on behalf of the white settler minority, had unilaterally declared independence, successive attempts to end the minority regime and reach a settlement had failed. The country was ravaged by a long-running civil war; the Commonwealth was divided as to what to do; the Tory right was against any 'sell out' of their 'kith and kin' to the African nationalists; and it was unwilling to support the renewal of sanctions. Carrington was determined to resolve the matter, but this meant taking Thatcher in a direction she did not wish to go, by recognizing that the leaders of the Rhodesian Patriotic Front, Joshua Nkomo and Robert Mugabe, for whom she had no sympathy, must be involved in any final settlement. The Rhodesia issue dominated the Commonwealth heads of government meeting at Lusaka in August 1979 where, at the beginning, Thatcher and such African leaders as Kenneth Kaunda of Zambia and Julius Nyerere of Tanzania were a long way apart. But Carrington persuaded her to accept an agreement whereby Britain would host a constitutional conference involving all interested parties, install a temporary governor, supervise a general election in which all Africans would vote, and police the transition to independence.

Thatcher was not wholly happy with the deal struck at Lusaka, but she left the conference more popular than when she had arrived; despite her misgivings, she defended it in public as offering the only way forward, and faced down the

Tory party's Rhodesia lobby. The constitutional conference, presided over by Carrington, took place at Lancaster House between September and December, and Thatcher again refused to support last-minute appeals on behalf of the white settlers. Instead she sent out Soames, as interim governor, even as the civil war was still raging; but he successfully oversaw an election held in February 1980, and two months later formally transferred power to an independent Zimbabwe. The result, and largely thanks to Carrington and Soames, was Thatcher's first triumph in foreign affairs, as the Rhodesian issue appeared to have been belatedly solved. Yet there was concern that the wrong man had won the election, for the Foreign Office much preferred Nkomo to Mugabe, believing he would be more conciliatory. But Mugabe won, and long after Thatcher had left power he would become increasingly intransigent and authoritarian. She, meanwhile, was never fully reconciled to the political fix she had agreed, later lamenting that Britain had sold out the white Rhodesian settlers for nothing more than a short-term deal. Nevertheless, at the time she had gone along with a very 'pragmatic' solution.

In dealing with the European Communities (EC), Thatcher was more intransigent, although not in the first instance successfully. In 1978 British membership had cost £800 million; the following year it was heading towards £1 billion. This was too much: Thatcher was becoming increasingly suspicious of the unelected and unaccountable Brussels bureaucracy; and these attitudes played well in the popular press, at a time when she needed some popularity. She demanded a substantial rebate in the British contribution, and at the meeting of the EC leaders in Dublin in November 1979 she subjected them to a hectoring and undiplomatic harangue the like of which none of them had heard before at such a gathering. She refused the eleventh-hour proposal of a £350 million cut, but agreed the matter should be discussed again at later meetings. In Luxembourg the following April the EC offer to Britain was increased to £760 million, and in May 1980 an outline settlement between Britain and the EC was negotiated by Carrington and Gilmour, which was a further improvement on the Luxembourg figure. Thatcher declared the terms unacceptable; but Carrington and Gilmour took the fight to the cabinet where, to her rage and dismay, they prevailed, and the terms of the agreement were accepted.

Thatcher's experiences at Lusaka and Dublin reinforced her low opinions of the African leaders of the Commonwealth and of the dominant Franco-German axis in the EC. From the beginning of her premiership she was also determined to challenge Moscow, and in more confrontational terms than the Foreign Office recommended. In June 1979 she met the Soviet prime minister, Alexi Kosygin, in Moscow, *en route* to the economic summit in Tokyo: she more than held her own with him. Six months later, the Soviets invaded Afghanistan, which Thatcher regarded as an even more blatant act of aggression than the occupation of Czechoslovakia eleven years before. But her attempts to urge a co-ordinated Western response, including a systematic boycott of the Olympic games to be held in Moscow the following year, met with little success. As an ardent transatlanticist Thatcher looked on Britain's relationship with the United States as more friendly and important than that with any other country; but she regarded President Jimmy Carter as weak and indecisive, and with no vision for America's future. Nevertheless, she sought to establish cordial relations in what would be the closing months of his one term of office. At the end of 1979, when Carter was mired in the Iran hostage crisis, she made a cheerleading visit to Washington; and while he regarded her as 'highly opinionated [and] strong willed',[4] he admired her leadership and loyalty.

Thatcher's great Anglo-American opportunity came when Ronald Reagan defeated Carter in the election of November 1980, and the following February she again flew to Washington as (almost) the first foreign head of government to see the newly inaugurated president. In many ways they were very different figures: he was sunny, genial, charming, relaxed, upbeat, and with little intellectual curiosity or command of policy detail; she was domineering, belligerent, confrontational, tireless, hyperactive, and with an unrivalled command of facts and figures. But the chemistry between them worked. Reagan had been grateful for her interest in him at a time when the British establishment refused to take him seriously; she agreed with him about the importance of creating wealth, cutting taxes, and building up stronger defences against Soviet Russia; and both believed in liberty and free-market freedom, and in the need to outface what Reagan would later call 'the evil empire'.[5] There were those in his administration who thought her policies were not working, while she worried that the president wanted to cut taxes by too much. But her visit was a huge success: she wowed Washington with her energy and glamour; she consolidated her rapport with the president; and it gave her a much-needed boost when her standing at home was at its nadir.

4

Victory Overseas, 1981–83

'It does no harm to throw the occasional man overboard, but it does not do much good if you are steering full speed ahead for the rocks.'

(Sir Ian Gilmour, 1981)[1]

'The Prime Minister, shortly after she came into office, received a soubriquet as "the Iron Lady". . . . In the next week or two, this House, the nation and the right honourable lady herself will learn of what metal she is made.'

(Enoch Powell in the House of Commons, 3 April 1982)

Summer of discontent

By the spring of 1981 it did not seem as though anything the Thatcher government was doing domestically was working. Stagflation was intensifying, in that prices and wages were still rising out of control, but so, too, was unemployment; and Howe's 1981 budget appeared to be making things worse, not better. Her chances of surviving until the next election, let alone of winning it, seemed minimal, and her opponents in cabinet, by then disparagingly known as the 'wets', were becoming increasingly vocal critics. For everything that Thatcher was doing, especially her determination to contemplate, with relative equanimity, massive rises in unemployment which in earlier decades would have been deemed unacceptable, was anathema to those 'one nation', paternalist Tories who formed the majority of her cabinet. To be sure, Whitelaw had pledged his loyalty, and Carrington was preoccupied with foreign affairs. But they were not indifferent to the wrenching social consequences of what Thatcher and Howe were doing to the economy, while Pym, Gilmour, Soames, Prior, Walker, and Heseltine were exercised by the government's lack of social compassion and its seeming indifference to the sufferings of ordinary people who, they believed, were being sacrificed on the misguided altar of monetarist dogma. They feared the social fabric of the nation was being subjected to unprecedented assaults, and during the spring and summer of 1981 their worst forebodings were borne out.

In the middle of April serious disturbances occurred in Brixton, a multiracial south London suburb with a history of poor police–community relations and high unemployment, especially among young black men. Nearly three hundred policemen and scores of people were injured, and twenty-eight buildings were destroyed or damaged by fire. These disorderly scenes were followed by protests at Toxteth in Liverpool in July, along with lesser troubles at Moss Side in Manchester, Handsworth in Birmingham, and Chapeltown in Leeds, and by another outburst in Brixton. To Thatcher's critics, this vindicated their view that the government's punitive economic policies, intensifying both depression and inflation rather than mitigating either, were placing an intolerable strain on the social fabric of the nation. For a time the mood in the Tory party was close to panic, and at the last cabinet meeting before the summer recess, held in late July 1981, the 'wets', including Heseltine, Pym, Gilmour, and Soames, expressed fears for the future of the country and the party, while the veteran Hailsham likened what was happening on the streets of Britain to what had occurred on the streets of Germany in the early 1930s. But Thatcher was unrepentant. She refused to concede that social deprivation and economic hardship were the cause of the riots: the destruction of property, the looting of shops, and the attacks on the police were crimes, and should be treated and punished as such.

The July cabinet was the high point of the 'wets'' attempt to force Thatcher to change course. But they had no real alternative policies to propose, and they were unwilling to contemplate the supreme act of disloyalty, namely collective resignation. Thatcher was more determined and decisive than they were and at the end of the summer she struck back. In January she had already sacked Norman St John Stevas, who had been leader of the Commons and minister for the arts, and in September she mopped up the 'wets'. She dismissed Gilmour, who had publicly criticized the government's economic policies; she got rid of Mark Carlisle, who had not done well at education; and she fired Soames, who had forfeited her confidence by his mishandling of the recent strike of civil servants. She also removed Prior from employment, where he had been insufficiently robust in his dealing with the trades unions, and exiled him to the Northern Ireland Office. In the ensuing reshuffle she moved Joseph to education; she made Nigel Lawson secretary of state for energy; Norman Tebbit replaced Prior at employment; and she brought in Cecil Parkinson as paymaster-general and Tory party chairman: all three new ministers held views closer to hers than the men they replaced. But although she had created a cabinet more to her liking, it did not improve the government's standing. In September 1981 the Tories were eight points behind Labour in the opinion polls, and three months later only 25 per cent of voters were satisfied with Thatcher's performance, making her the most unpopular premier since polling had begun.

Although there was little evidence for it at the time, events were beginning to move Thatcher's way. There had been another massive increase in oil prices at the end of 1979, which further fuelled inflation; but the United Kingdom would soon be drawing its own supplies from beneath the North Sea, and would become a net exporter, which would increase government revenue, thereby making possible further tax cuts. Moreover, the recession bottomed out just after the economists had published their letter in *The Times*. Between 1981 and 1989 real growth would average 3.2 per cent a year, compared with sixteen months of negative growth during 1980 and 1981; and by 1983 inflation would be down to less than 5 per cent. Meanwhile Callaghan had resigned as Labour leader, and in November 1980 was replaced by Foot. He proved no match for Thatcher at prime minister's questions, where her unrivalled command of detail invariably punctured his vague and often ill-informed verbosity, and Labour began a march to the left that would render it unelectable for more than a decade. Soon after Foot became leader, the disaffected Labour quartet of Roy Jenkins, Shirley Williams, David Owen, and William Rodgers established the breakaway Social Democratic Party (SDP). As in earlier recessions, at the end of the nineteenth century and during the interwar years, Thatcher would enjoy the advantage of a divided opposition, and under Britain's first past the post electoral system this would virtually guarantee her next two election victories.

These uncovenanted domestic benefits were accompanied by the beginnings of significant changes in the international order. The Russian invasion of Afghanistan in 1979 may have caused Thatcher short-term political embarrassment, but it was a deeply misguided overseas venture that would eventually prove fatal to the continued existence of the Soviet Union. At the same time, there was growing opposition in Poland to continued Soviet rule, led by Lech Wałęsa, who was the leader of the recently established trades union Solidarity, based in the Gdansk shipyards; and while Thatcher was vehemently opposed to organized, anti-capitalist labour militancy in Britain, she was very happy to encourage it when it took the form of anti-communist labour militancy elsewhere. Moreover, in 1979, the former archbishop of Kraków, who a year earlier had been elected Pope John Paul II, had made a triumphant return visit to Poland, when millions turned out to attend his speeches and his masses, which the authorities were powerless to prevent. The iron curtain was beginning to crack, and the deaths of Alexi Kosygin in 1980, of Leonid

Brezhnev two years later, and of Yuri Andropov in 1984, suggested the days of Moscow's Politburo gerontocracy were numbered, and that there might be the prospect of some sort of East–West détente.

Yet none of these developments was to Thatcher's immediate political advantage. The 1981 Conservative Party conference, held in the aftermath of her cabinet reshuffle, took place in an atmosphere of crisis and panic, intensified by the worst poll ratings of any government since 1945, by another emergency rise in interest rates to 16 per cent, and by a powerful intervention by Heath, calling for a national recovery package to tackle unemployment. Soon after, Shirley Williams overturned a Tory majority of 19,272 to win Crosby for the SDP, at which point it seemed as though no Conservative seat in the country was safe; and in March 1982 Roy Jenkins, the SDP leader, won Glasgow Hillhead, and for a time was widely regarded as the man who would become the next prime minister. Late in 1981 Thatcher claimed that 'we are through the worst';[2] but, three years since her election victory, the prospects of a second Tory win looked very slim. By the spring of 1982 the three major parties, namely the Conservatives, Labour, and the Liberal–SDP Alliance, were at level pegging in the polls, each likely to win between 30 and 33 per cent of the votes. The surge of the Alliance, combined with the Labour lurch to the left, and the Tories' continued unpopularity, meant that most commentators were predicting a hung parliament after the next election, which would have spelt Thatcher's doom. But in April 1982 Argentina invaded the Falkland Islands, and her political fortunes would soon be miraculously transformed.

The Falklands War

The Falkland Islands are located in the south Atlantic, 8000 miles from the United Kingdom, and 300 miles from the southern extremity of Argentina. They had been acquired by Britain in 1833, as a significant staging post between the Atlantic and Pacific oceans; and they were settled by sheep farmers who were fiercely loyal to the crown. But British possession had been repeatedly disputed by France and Spain, and especially by Argentina, and by the 1970s the Falklands were regarded in the Foreign Office as one of those embarrassing residues of empire, along with Rhodesia, Gibraltar, and Hong Kong, of which they wished to be rid. The preferred diplomatic solution was to cede sovereignty to Argentina, in return for which the British government would continue to administer the islands on behalf of the settlers. Such a 'leaseback' scheme was favoured by Carrington, and in November 1980 he sent Nicholas Ridley, then a junior minister, to the Falklands to try to persuade the 1800 islanders to accept it. But they were determined to remain British subjects, and Ridley returned to London empty-handed. Meanwhile, right-wing Tories, already alarmed by what had happened in Rhodesia, deplored the idea of another 'sell-out', and the leaseback scheme was quietly dropped.

As a result the Falklands were no longer a high priority at the Foreign Office; but they soon reappeared on the very different agenda of the Ministry of Defence. In her reshuffle of January 1981 Thatcher had replaced Pym with John Nott, whom she believed would be more sympathetic to cutting the costs of the armed forces as part of the government's policy of reducing public expenditure. Nott instituted a review of Britain's future military needs, which reported in June and was particularly harsh on the Royal Navy, on the grounds that a future large-scale war at sea was highly unlikely. He proposed a reduction in the number of aircraft carriers from three to two, and of frigates and destroyers from fifty-nine to fifty. He also announced that the ice-patrol ship HMS *Endurance*, which intercepted Argentinian intelligence, and affirmed Britain's continuing interest and presence in the south Atlantic, would be withdrawn. These decisions, which Thatcher supported, were taken as a signal by the military junta then in power in Argentina, led by General Leopoldo Galtieri, that the United Kingdom was no longer seriously committed to the Falklands. In January 1982 the junta began making their invasion plans, and although the British government would soon learn about them, there was nothing they could do to prevent them being carried out. Carrington and Thatcher urged President Reagan to try to persuade Galtieri to stay his hand. But his efforts were unavailing, the invasion duly place, and by 2 April the Argentinian flag was flying over Port Stanley, the capital of the Falklands, instead of the Union Jack.

The loss of the Falklands was the greatest international humiliation suffered by the United Kingdom since the Suez fiasco of 1956. After a stormy Commons session and a critical meeting of Tory back-benchers, Carrington resigned, although he bore less responsibility than Nott, whose defence cuts had emboldened the Argentinians to invade, and than Thatcher, who had failed to take the subject seriously until it was too late. She was now faced with a near-insoluble dilemma. As the 'Iron Lady', who regularly proclaimed her courage, conviction, and consistency, and repeatedly insisted that conflict was better than compromise, she could not allow the Argentinians to get away with such a blatant act of aggression, and had she done so she would have been obliged to resign. But the alternative, namely mounting a long-distance and hugely expensive military campaign to win the Falklands back, was an enterprise fraught with risk, and if it failed then she would also be finished as prime minister. Her resolve stiffened by Admiral Sir Henry Leach, Thatcher instructed the defence staff and the service chiefs to assemble a naval task force. It set sail from Portsmouth on 5 and 6 April, led by HMS *Hermes* and including HMS *Invincible*, the same aircraft carrier Nott had earlier resolved to sell to Australia.

Thatcher appointed a small war cabinet, consisting of Whitelaw (he had commanded tanks in Normandy in 1944), Parkinson (for his smooth presentational skills on television), Nott (as minister of defence), and Pym (who had replaced Carrington at the Foreign Office). She was also well served by Admiral Sir Terence Lewin as chief of the defence staff; by Sir Anthony Parsons, Britain's permanent representative to the UN, who carried a resolution at the Security Council condemning Argentina's invasion, which effectively gave her cover for sending the task force; and by Sir Nicholas Henderson, the British ambassador to Washington, who persistently lobbied the Reagan administration, and put the government's case in a succession of television interviews. But, to Thatcher's annoyance, Reagan refused to come out in her support, claiming that the United States was friends with both Britain and Argentina, while his secretary of state, Alexander Haig, sought to broker a diplomatic solution, and spent the next few weeks shuttling between London, New York, Washington, and Buenos Aires. Moreover, Jeanne Kirkpatrick, America's permanent representative to the UN, thought the United States should remain friendly with the countries of Latin America rather than support Britain. But the secretary of defense, Caspar Weinberger, took a very different view, covertly providing the task force with essential military assistance, including the use of America's Ascension Island base in the mid-Atlantic for refuelling, the accelerated provision of Sidewinder missiles, and unprecedented access to US intelligence.

The six weeks that it took for the task force to reach the south Atlantic allowed ample time for a negotiated settlement, but Thatcher was determined that such well-intentioned peacemaking would not pre-empt the military victory she believed was the only outcome the British people would accept. She also recognized that she would forfeit international support if she appeared too inflexible; but, fortunately for her, the Argentinians were more intransigent than she was, and twice rejected peace packages put forward by the Americans. Yet still Reagan declined to give Britain the endorsement Thatcher wanted, although he knew that if she failed in the Falklands, he would almost certainly lose his staunchest European ally. On 2 May the British submarine HMS *Conqueror* sank the Argentinian cruiser *General Belgrano*, with the loss of 323 lives; two days later the Argentines sank the British destroyer HMS *Sheffield*, killing twenty of her crew. On 12 May the requisitioned Cunard liner *Queen Elizabeth 2* set sail from Southampton carrying 3,000 further troops, and on 21 May the first amphibious landings on the Falklands took place. Once battle was joined the British lost two frigates, a destroyer, a transport ship, and a troopship, and there was renewed pressure from the United States and at the UN for a cessation of hostilities. But Parsons vetoed a Security Council resolution calling for a ceasefire, while Thatcher gave Reagan short shrift when he urged magnanimity. Meanwhile, the conscript Argentinian army evinced little appetite for battle, and on 14 June British troops recaptured Port Stanley. The following day more than 11,000 Argentine soldiers surrendered and, soon after, Galtieri fell from power.

Although Thatcher gave full credit to the service chiefs who had planned the campaign and the men who had fought her battles, she was the supreme architect and beneficiary of their victory. She had taken huge military and political risks, but her resolution and determination had never wavered. She had indeed shown herself to be the 'Iron Lady', and as she welcomed 'our boys' back to Portsmouth, and took the salute at the victory parade, her domestic political prospects were dramatically transformed. In the summer of 1981 she had been the most unpopular prime minister since polling began, facing a divided cabinet, a demoralized party, and an SDP which seemed inexorably on the rise. But neither Foot nor Jenkins had shone during the war as their respective party leaders; by July 1982 her own approval ratings had doubled to 51 per cent; and her position suddenly became unassailable. She had stood up to aggression, faced down a dictator, defended liberty, and safeguarded the rule of law. No other Western leader could claim as much, and this made Thatcher the darling of the American right, even as it was bad news for the old men in the Kremlin. She had saved Britain's honour, avenged the failure of Suez, reversed national decline, and made the country great again. 'We have ceased to be a nation in retreat', she proclaimed.

> We have instead a new-found confidence—born in the economic battles at home, and tested and found true 8,000 miles away . . . Britain found herself again in the South Atlantic, and will not look back from the victory she has won.[3]

Such were Thatcher's claims; but the causes and consequences of the Falklands War were more complex and contradictory than that. British losses were relatively low, but she wept openly and often when told of the latest casualties, and wrote to the families of all the bereaved. Although the commission of inquiry into the causes of the war, led by Lord Franks, and reporting in January 1983, would exonerate Thatcher from any blame, her government clearly bore some responsibility for the Argentinian invasion. The cost of the conflict, and the longer-term expenses of replacing ships and equipment, combined with the additional outlay for constructing a 'Fortress Falklands', and for keeping British troops permanently stationed there, amounted to £3 billion, a significant sum for a government determined to cut public spending, even if it was funded out of the contingency reserve. Had Nott's proposed defence cuts, which Thatcher had endorsed, been implemented more promptly, she would probably have lacked the resources to assemble the task force; and the plans to slash naval spending, which had helped precipitate the crisis, were quietly shelved. For all Thatcher's insistence that victory was an unalloyed national triumph, it would have been impossible without the American assistance authorized by Weinberger. And was it really the case that the recovery of a few small islands at what seemed like the end of the world, of which most people in Britain had never heard, from a corrupt Latin American government and its incompetent military, had at one single stroke arrested decades of national decline?

Towards a second term

At the time little attention was paid to these qualifications and questions: the war had been won, which was all that mattered. Even Reagan had finally climbed off the fence. On 8 June 1982, during a pre-arranged visit to London, when the battle in the south Atlantic was reaching its climax, he saluted the 'young men' who were not just 'fighting for Britain', but for 'the belief that armed aggression must not be allowed to succeed and that people must participate in the decisions of government under the rule of law'.[4] With Anglo-American relations restored, and with the Argentinian surrender a few days later, it was widely recognized that Thatcher would win the next general election. But to ask for a dissolution in the aftermath of victory might seem a cynical attempt to cash in on it. Instead, she insisted that her government was intent on applying the lessons of the south Atlantic to problems nearer home, of which the economy remained the most pressing and persistent. Howe had declared that the recession had ended during the third quarter of 1981; but growth during 1982 was minimal, while industrial output was the lowest since 1965. Unemployment had reached three million, and despite the boost given by what would be termed the 'Falklands factor', no British government had ever been re-elected with so many people out of work. There were also renewed calls from trades unions and employers for the cabinet to take more action to stimulate the economic recovery that was constantly being promised but never actually arrived.

Unsurprisingly, the government's preferred yardstick for measuring the success of its economic policies was not unemployment, but inflation. By the end of 1982 it was down to 5 per cent, which enabled Howe to cut interest rates to 9 per cent. The heavy shedding of manpower began to yield higher productivity in those parts of the manufacturing economy that had survived, and in his 1982 budget, delivered just before the Falklands invasion, he was able, while keeping a tight rein on public spending, to offer some targeted incentives to growth, among them more free ports, and an increase in the number of enterprise zones. Economic activity continued to pick up, albeit slowly, and in the spring of 1983 Howe made some modest tax concessions, not by cutting the basic rate again, but by raising personal thresholds and allowances, increasing child benefit, and restoring the cuts he had made the previous year in unemployment benefit. By then the government could claim its economic strategy was working: inflation was being driven down, making possible a real economic recovery built around productive jobs. Yet by the summer of 1983 gross domestic product would still be 4 per cent lower than in 1979, and manufacturing output 17 per cent down. This was a deeper and more protracted depression than any other European nation endured, and it left parts of south Wales, lowland Scotland, and the north of England devastated. Like the Tory 'wets' the opposition parties complained that Thatcher lacked compassion; her retort was that toughness and resolution had won out in the Falklands, and would eventually win out at home as well.

Success in the south Atlantic also emboldened Thatcher to push ahead in her assault on organized labour. In 1982 the new employment secretary, Tebbit, carried a measure which ended the privileged status granted to the unions by the Liberal government in the aftermath of the Taff Vale judgment of 1906. They would no longer be immune from civil suits arising out of unlawful trades disputes, and the definition of illegal action was considerably extended. Tebbit's legislation also increased restrictions on the operation of closed shops, made it easier for employers to sack persistent trouble-makers, and provided funds to finance union ballots. These terms were denounced by the TUC and the Labour opposition, but public opinion was in favour; so were many trades unionists, and the ever-upward trend in unemployment weakened organized labour still further. Long-running strikes by railwaymen and NHS workers ended in defeat for the unions, and workers at British Leyland accepted a pay offer their leaders had urged them to reject. A second distinctive policy began to take shape in 1982, namely privatization. By October that year 370,000 families had availed themselves of the 'right to buy' their council houses that had been established in 1980, and the government drew up plans to sell off British Telecom (BT). They would not be implemented until after the election, but Britoil, which had been established by Benn to give the state a stake in North Sea production, was privatized in November 1982, raising £334 million.

'We are only in our first term', Thatcher told the party conference the previous month, 'but already we have done more to roll back the frontiers of socialism than any previous Conservative government'.[5] There was another arena where socialism had to be fought, and that concerned the continued existence of Britain's nuclear deterrent. As a vehement anti-communist, Thatcher believed that such weapons were the only way of ensuring world peace, and were also an emblem of the nation's continued power and independence. Soon after taking office her government had agreed to replace Britain's ageing Polaris weapons with Trident missiles, manufactured in the United States. In January 1982 the Americans offered an even more sophisticated version of Trident, and Thatcher drew on her close relationship with Reagan to acquire it on very favourable terms. In return she was willing to let the Americans deploy cruise missiles at military bases in Britain, but these actions and decisions brought back to life the long-dormant Campaign for Nuclear Disarmament (CND), which made common cause with the Labour leadership, who under Foot had embraced unilateralism. Thatcher denounced CND and excoriated Foot for advocating what she had already described as 'unilateral surrender';[6] and in January 1983 she removed Nott from the Ministry of Defence, where his lacklustre performance had not impressed her during the

Falklands War, and replaced him with the more flamboyant and belligerent (and ambitious) Heseltine.

By this time Thatcher was under increasing pressure from her party managers to decide on a date for the general election, which they were confident she would now win. While her approval ratings had been at record lows she had given little thought to the possibility that she might be returned to power. Before the Falklands War it seemed unlikely she would be re-elected, and the conflict preoccupied her to the exclusion of all else until the autumn of 1982. Only then did she realize there might be a second term, but after the burdens and anxieties of the summer she was more tired than she would admit, and she did not give serious consideration to what she might do if re-elected. When she addressed the party conference in October she received a rousing, flag-waving reception, but her speech was light on detail, beyond signalling the privatization of Britoil and BT, celebrating the sale of council houses, and promising to leave the health service alone. But the omens were good: the Tories had been solidly ahead in the polls for months; the SDP had peaked and was on the way down; and Labour seemed in complete disarray. The local elections held on 5 May 1983 were reassuring, as the Conservatives gained 128 council seats in England and Wales. Thatcher eventually settled for an election on 9 June; and although she had no well-founded fear of losing, she took the precaution of clearing up her personal belongings in 10 Downing Street in case she had to depart in a hurry.

The Tory manifesto was little more specific than Thatcher's conference speech had been six months before: it committed to the privatization of BT, British Airways, and 'substantial parts' of British Steel, British Shipbuilders, and British Leyland; and it promised the further tightening of trade union law. But these were scarcely surprising proposals, and the only novelty was the promised abolition of the Greater London Council (GLC), and of the six large English metropolitan counties. This failure to put forward a well-worked-out and radical programme would leave the government struggling to regain some sense of purpose during its second term. But, compared with Labour's irresponsible and ill-judged offering, it seemed a minor masterpiece of realism and sagacity. Rightly described by Gerald Kaufman as 'the longest suicide note in history',[7] Labour's proposals gave the impression that the last four years had not happened: extending nationalization, massively increasing public spending, restoring the trade union privileges recently taken away, withdrawing from the EC, and embracing unilateral nuclear disarmament. Thatcher denounced and ridiculed these proposals, and the whole Tory campaign was built more around her than any specific policies. She dominated the media and trounced her television interviewers; and compared with her torrential energy, impassioned conviction, and undoubted achievements, Foot and Jenkins seemed long-winded, old-fashioned, and out of touch.

The outcome of the election was never seriously in doubt: the only unresolved issue was just how great Thatcher's victory would be. In the end it was 144 seats over all the other parties, which meant she became the only twentieth-century Tory leader to increase her Commons preponderance from one general election to the next. She held onto her own seat, Finchley, with a reduced share of the vote but a larger majority, of 9,314. Labour had descended into fratricidal unelectability, and Foot resigned the party leadership in October 1983; while the Liberal–SDP Alliance, by splitting the opposition vote, had done more to contribute to Thatcher's victory than to its own electoral prospects (it gained 25.4 per cent of the vote but only twenty-three seats), and Jenkins fell on his sword soon after. In reconstructing her cabinet after the election Thatcher's main aim was to get rid of Pym, whose hangdog looks and lugubrious manner had incensed her during the Falklands War. She sacked him, and he never held office again. She wished to replace him as foreign secretary with Parkinson, who as party chairman had helped deliver her election victory; but he revealed privately to her that he had fathered a child by a woman who was not his wife, and she gave the job to Howe instead, consoling Parkinson with the lesser post of secretary of state for trade and industry. To follow Howe at the exchequer, she appointed Lawson, who had previously been secretary of state for energy; and after she had given Whitelaw a viscountcy he left the Commons and the Home Office (where he was replaced by Leon Brittan) to become lord president of the council and leader of the House of Lords.

Despite her triumph at the polls Thatcher was never popular with most of the electorate, and studies showed that her values were not widely shared. In 1979 the Conservatives had won with only 43.9 per cent of the vote, one of the lowest showings achieved by a victorious party in modern times; but, four years later, Thatcher's hugely swollen Commons majority rested on a lesser share of the popular vote: down to 42.4 per cent. In Wales, Scotland, and large parts of the north of England, where industry had collapsed and unemployment was so high, her writ scarcely ran, and in some ways, she was only prime minister of the south-east of England and the rural constituencies. Yet that was all Thatcher had needed to win, and she increasingly came to believe, in the aftermath of the Falklands, that she was invincible, and even, perhaps, infallible, convinced that will-power and determination were what was needed to secure success, and that she alone could provide them. In dealing with her colleagues she would become even more hectoring and overbearing; her outfits and her demeanour would become increasingly regal; and she began to use the royal 'we', as when she observed, apropos of the Falklands War, that 'We're very grateful that we were in government when it happened',[8] and later when she declared, on the birth of her grandson, Michael Thatcher, 'We have become a grandmother'.[9] These were signs of mounting hubris; and sooner or later, nemesis would surely follow.

5

Enemies Within, 1983–86

'The 1983 general election result was the single most devastating defeat ever inflicted upon democratic socialism in Britain.'

(Margaret Thatcher, 1993)[1]

'I was up to my neck with Scargill. We broadly merged the miners' strike and the GLC campaign . . . I always thought the miners could defeat Thatcher.'

(Ken Livingstone, former leader of the GLC)[2]

Alone of all her sex

Nevertheless, for the time being Thatcher's position was unassailable: she was conquering inflation, she had vanquished Galtieri, and she had won two general elections. She had seen off Foot and Jenkins (and their successors, Neil Kinnock and David Owen, would fare little better). Reagan in the United States and François Mitterrand in France had both been elected presidents after she had become prime minister, and within a few months the advent to power of Helmut Schmidt in Germany and of Andropov in Russia meant they, too, would be her juniors. As a result Thatcher would soon play an increasingly senior and confident role on the global stage. A further indication of her unique position was the many names by which she was becoming known, and the varied, indeed contradictory, attitudes and identities, fears and fantasies they suggested. She was the 'Good Housewife' or the 'Grocer's Daughter' (or 'La Fille d'Épicier', according to Mitterrand's predecessor, Giscard d'Estaing). She was the 'Iron Lady' or the 'Warrior Queen', or even 'Britannia' or 'Gloriana'. To her admirers she was 'Maggie' or 'the Blessed Margaret' (a nickname coined by Stevas, along with 'Tina', for 'There Is No Alternative') or, less flatteringly, 'the Great She-Elephant' (according to Julian Critchley); but to her opponents she was 'That Bloody Woman' or 'Attila the Hen'. No male prime minister had ever been known by so many admiring and vituperative sobriquets. Was this sexism, or celebrity, or both?

For the whole of her public life Thatcher was a woman in an overwhelmingly man's world, and she had only reached the top by seeming to suppress the tender, nurturing, emollient qualities often associated with wives and mothers, and by demonstrating the assertive, domineering, and aggressive attributes more commonly associated with alpha males. She was combative and competitive, she scorned consensus and compromise, and she constantly emphasized her will-power, determination, tirelessness, and courage. She regarded her dealings with foreign heads of government, with her own cabinet, and with the civil service as trials of strength she was determined to win; and the same was true of her performances in the Commons, especially at question time, where she eventually achieved an unrivalled mastery. As President Carter's national security adviser, Zbigniew Brzezinski, put it in a comment that may say as much about him as about her: 'In her presence you pretty quickly forget that she's a woman. She doesn't strike me as being a very female type'.[3] Indeed, as both party leader and prime minister she seemed to be not so much a 'real woman', but much more of a 'male type'—hence the puppet caricature of her, created for the satirical television programme *Spitting Image*, where she was dressed in a man's business suit and wearing a tie, and where her demeanour was unfailingly harsh and severe.

It was this abrasiveness that led Barbara Castle to complain that Thatcher was completely insensitive to the particular difficulties that ordinary women faced when 'struggling to deal with a home, earn a wage, deal with an elderly parent . . . and sickness in the family'.[4] She had even less sympathy with the left-wing female activists who protested at the arrival of American missiles at Greenham Common, and feminism was a cause and a creed to which she was wholly unattracted. She claimed to be viscerally opposed to any form of politics built around adversarial group identities, and she preferred to think of people as individuals, rather than as collectivities going into battle to achieve shared goals and objectives—indeed, she went further, and at one point claimed that 'there is no such thing as society', though she went on to qualify her statement by adding, 'There are individual men and women, and there are families. . . . It's our duty to look after ourselves and then, also to look after our neighbour'.[5] As someone who believed, like her father, in personal self-improvement, and making the best of one's talents, she felt no inclination to put herself out for other women; she had no time for positive discrimination or affirmative action; and she regarded the very idea of the mutually supporting sisterhood of 'Women's Libbers' as incomprehensible. Indeed, during her eleven years of prime ministerial power only one other woman sat in Thatcher's cabinet, Baroness Young, who was briefly leader of the Lords from 1981 to 1983, when she was demoted to being a minister of state at the Foreign Office to make way for the ennobled Whitelaw. At no time during her premiership did any other female sit on her Commons front bench.

Nevertheless, there was one woman with whom Thatcher had to do business throughout her prime ministership—a woman, moreover, who had been at the very top in domestic and international politics for the best part of three decades before she entered 10 Downing Street, and who would continue in that position for at least as long after she left it, namely Queen Elizabeth II. Although born within a few months of each other, the prime minister and her sovereign were never natural soul mates in the way that Thatcher and Reagan were. They came from different worlds, culturally, socially, and geographically; unlike Thatcher, the Queen was an instinctive paternalist in domestic matters, preferring consensus and compromise to conflict and confrontation; and in foreign affairs she was devoted to the Commonwealth, for whose leaders Thatcher had little respect. In 1986 the *Sunday Times* would run a story, deliberately leaked by the Queen's press secretary, that she was 'dismayed' by her 'uncaring' prime minister,[6] which Buckingham Palace never explicitly denied. In public Thatcher was exaggeratedly deferential to her sovereign, curtseying more deeply than any other woman; but in private she could not hide her nervousness and insecurities, sitting on the edge of her seat and rarely seeking royal advice. So, while relations between premier and monarch were scrupulously correct, they were never warm or friendly.

Yet Thatcher also appeared in a variety of quintessentially womanly guises, one of which was as a 'de-eroticised' female,[7] devoid of sexual attraction or allure. She was feared or denounced as a virago or a fishwife, living in a permanent state of outrage, quarrelsomeness, and bad temper, and making the most stout-hearted men feel inadequate and apprehensive in her presence. Alternatively, she was the fierce headmistress keeping an unruly class in order; the dragon sister on the hospital ward ensuring that the male patients took their medicine; or the stern nanny teaching the boys to eat their vegetables. That was how she behaved when chairing cabinet meetings, announcing at the beginning of each item for discussion the conclusion that she wanted reached; and that was how she treated the briefings from ministers and civil servants, returning them peppered with comments, underlinings, and question marks. In yet another guise she was a latter-day Queen Boudicca, urging her troops into battle, who delighted in donning combat gear or being photographed in a British army tank. Or she was Lady Bracknell, a century on, for whom the handbag was an instrument of gendered aggression, rather than an essential repository for make-up and other female necessities. Time and again Thatcher made it plain that she took a dim view of the male species: 'If you want something said', she once observed, 'ask a man. If you want something done, ask a woman'.[8]

But Thatcher also took trouble to present herself as appealing and alluring to the opposite sex. She was always impeccably coiffured; her eyes were sky blue, her skin was clear, and her complexion fair; she applied carmine lipstick in considerable quantities; and she invariably wore high-heeled shoes to draw attention to her elegant legs. She took great care with her clothes, often changing her outfits several times a day, and preferring well-tailored suits in strong colours. She also exploited her gender, treating her cabinet colleagues in a way which no male prime minister could have done: brushing fluff from their shirt collars, straightening their ties, and buttoning (but not unbuttoning) their jackets. Even in the Commons she would occasionally play the feminine ingénue. On one occasion when Foot offered to take Thatcher to dinner every time the government reneged on a promise, she replied that it was 'a lady's prerogative to say "no"'.[9] During the Falklands War she came to feel a particularly strong affinity with the men in uniform, and she also had a weakness for handsome males of a certain age, who stood up straight and wore well-cut suits, who may have reminded her of Denis's earlier 'style and dash', and of which type Cecil Parkinson was a conspicuous example. Conservative men such as Alan Clark found Thatcher's combination of political authority and sex appeal extremely attractive, and she knew it.

Thatcher was also the beneficiary of the still-prevailing code of male gallantry which meant that few of her colleagues or adversaries were willing to stand up to her, or pay her out in her own confrontational coin. One of her back-bench critics,

Critchley, admitted that Tory men had 'been brought up to believe that it's extremely rude to shout back at women';[10] while Kinnock conceded that, as Labour leader, he felt inhibited at prime minister's questions from being too aggressive. Thatcher also cried in public, which was hardly how an 'Iron Lady' might have been expected to behave: when she failed to get her way at Lusaka during some preliminary discussions over Rhodesia; when her son, Mark, disappeared for six days during a trans-Sahara motor rally; and when she made her last journey from Downing Street to Buckingham Palace to resign as prime minister. Above all she remained the good housewife, though this was no more than a residual activity. 'The home', she once observed, 'should be the centre but not the boundary of a woman's life',[11] and that was what she made 10 Downing Street. She took great trouble in selecting the pictures for the public rooms, she borrowed silver from Lord Brownlow, the nearby Grantham grandee, and she treated her personal and domestic staff with a kindness and consideration she conspicuously failed to display when dealing with her male colleagues.

As the undisputed alpha female of her generation Margaret Thatcher was thus a bundle of gendered contradictions, which by sheer force of personality she concealed and carried off with sustained bravura and conviction. She was also supported, throughout her time at Downing Street, by a husband whose money had made her public career possible, and who self-effacingly subordinated his life to hers, yet who could also order her to bed when she had stayed up working too late. But while she was, after her fashion, a devoted and appreciative wife, she was always a more distant than a nurturing mother. Carol, of whom she did not think much, went off to make a career in Australia; while Mark, on whom she doted, was packed off to Dallas in Texas after some controversial involvement in arms dealing in the Middle East. Two quotations illustrate the paradoxes Thatcher denied and the inconsistencies she exploited which made her the remarkable woman of power she eventually became. At the end of the Falklands War she held a dinner at 10 Downing Street for the senior officers who had contributed most to the victory. Their wives were invited to the post-prandial reception, and at the end of the meal Thatcher stood up and said, 'Gentlemen, shall we join the ladies?'.[12] Some time after, President Mitterrand, who did not make his predecessor's mistake of treating her as a grocer's daughter, described Thatcher in very different terms, declaring that she combined 'the eyes of Caligula and the mouth of Marilyn Monroe'.[13]

Hard times

Despite her commanding Commons majority, and a cabinet she had remade in her own image, Thatcher's second term did not begin well. Having sacked Pym, she hoped the Commons might make him speaker; but MPs opted for Bernard Weatherill instead. The Queen's speech, setting out the government's legislative programme, was lacklustre, with few concrete or original proposals, and no radical or coherent agenda. The decision to bestow hereditary peerages on Whitelaw and on George Thomas, the outgoing speaker, seemed anachronistic and quixotic: there had been no such creations since 1964, and as Whitelaw's children were all daughters, and Thomas was unmarried, neither title would be passed on to the next generation. (Thatcher also ennobled Harold Macmillan in 1984, as earl of Stockton; and that title would pass on his death to his grandson.) Her promotion of Gow to the post of minister of state for housing, and his replacement as Thatcher's parliamentary private secretary by the austere and ungregarious Michael Alison, combined with a significant intake of new MPs, meant that she was less in touch with back-bench opinion during her second term than in her first. In July 1983 the new chancellor, Lawson, was compelled to announce a £500 million package of emergency spending cuts, to reassure the City there would be no loosening of monetary policy; the cuts fell heavily on defence and health, displeasing both the right and the left. Meanwhile, and despite Thatcher's oft-repeated claim that the recession was over, unemployment continued to rise.

There were other early indications of second-term frailty and fallibility. Thatcher went into hospital in August 1983, for an operation to repair a detached retina, and then took an unheard-of two weeks' holiday in Switzerland. The Tory party conference was overshadowed by revelations concerning Parkinson's extra-marital affair and love child, and he was compelled to resign from the cabinet (and was replaced at trade and industry by Tebbit). But Parkinson was not the only political friend who caused Thatcher embarrassment that autumn. In late September, she had again visited Reagan in Washington in the hope of devising a common policy for dealing with Soviet Russia. The following month, and unknown to Thatcher, Reagan agreed to a request from the Organization of Eastern Caribbean States to intervene on the island of Grenada, where the prime minister, Maurice Bishop, had been killed in a left-wing coup, and on 25 October he dispatched American troops. But Grenada was a Commonwealth country, the Queen was its head of state, and Thatcher was furious that the president had not consulted or informed her before authorizing the invasion. Moreover, the new foreign secretary, Howe, had told the Commons on the previous day that there was no such American plan. Far from being Reagan's partner, Thatcher seemed more like his poodle. She felt let down and humiliated not to have been taken into his confidence, and this was the worst rift of their partnership.

The year 1983 did not end well, with serious protests at Greenham Common, following the arrival of the first American cruise missiles to be based in Europe, which seemed further evidence of the United Kingdom's craven subordination to the United States. Nor did 1984 begin more auspiciously. In January, and at Thatcher's urging, Howe banned, by means of an order in council, the existence of trades unions at the Government Communications Headquarters, the intercept centre located outside Cheltenham. Intelligence personnel, the prime minister insisted, should not be in a position to endanger national security by taking industrial action; but the decision was deeply controversial, and the government was criticized for being high-handed and authoritarian, and for mounting yet another assault on organized labour. Two months later, in his first budget, Lawson sought to further his predecessor's policy of moving from direct to indirect taxation, and of favouring business, by raising personal thresholds, extending VAT, and slashing corporation tax: but such regressive measures led to criticism that he was more interested in helping the rich than assisting the poor. Meanwhile, there were complaints outside and inside the Conservative Party that a government which had spent millions of pounds to win back the far-off Falklands was unwilling to spend lesser sums to alleviate the great and growing social problems at home.

By this time the public mood was again turning against Thatcher. In May 1984 the Conservatives suffered significant reverses at the local elections; the following month Labour gained fifteen seats in the European parliament elections, and the SDP captured the safe Tory seat of Portsmouth at a by-election. Pym published a 'one nation' critique of the government entitled *The Politics of Consent* and, on the eve of the summer recess, Thatcher made an unimpressive reply to the first no-confidence motion moved by Kinnock since becoming Labour leader. With unemployment at well over three million, and still rising, she bowed to pressure by appointing the businessman David Young, ennobled as Lord Young of Graffham, to be the so-called 'minister for jobs'. At the party conference held in Brighton in October, two issues dominated, and neither suggested the government was in full control. The attempt to blow up the Grand Hotel by the IRA killed five people and seriously injured another thirty-four, and made plain that the Northern Ireland 'troubles' were no nearer to being solved. Thatcher (who was the target of the bombers) was lucky to escape with her life, and made a courageous defence of freedom and liberty in her conference speech, which she insisted on delivering later the same day. But most of it was devoted to an attempt, which did not entirely convince, to show that she cared deeply about the problems and consequences of unemployment. Once again the 'one nation' Tories protested that the government was callously indifferent to the plight of the unemployed. There was also a sterling crisis in January 1985 which compelled Lawson to raise interest rates to 14 per cent.

In the same month Thatcher's alma mater refused to grant her an honorary degree—an unprecedented snub, since all her Oxford-educated predecessors, from Attlee to Heath, had been so recognized. The university had changed her life, and Somerville had elected her to an honorary fellowship in 1970, when she became education secretary. But she had been dismayed by the widespread student protests during her term of office, she had been annoyed by the letter written by the 364 economists in 1981, and she deplored what she regarded as the incorrigible hostility of academics to the enterprise culture of wealth creation. Moreover, the cuts in public spending during her first administration had hit higher education hard, not only in the humanities but in pure science as well. She also wanted universities to contribute more to economic growth, and was determined to make them more publicly accountable. Since 1945 it had been customary for Oxford to award honorary degrees to its prime-ministerial alumni during their first year of office, but in Thatcher's case the matter was not seriously raised until late in 1984, by which time academic opinion had turned deeply hostile. Her supporters also underestimated the local opposition (as with the 'milk-snatcher' episode, the staff work was poor), and pressed ahead regardless; but convocation, the university's governing body, rejected the proposal by 738 votes to 319.

Thatcher never forgave Oxford for inflicting such a humiliating slight.

Still, the issue of unemployment remained, and Lawson was obliged to dress up his March 1985 budget as being 'for jobs'. He reduced national insurance and put additional money into youth training schemes, but the result was generally regarded as uninspiring. At the county council elections held in May the Tories lost heavily to the Liberal–SDP Alliance, and again found themselves trailing third in the opinion polls. Three months later the government lost the previously safe seat of Brecon and Radnor to the Alliance, and the Conservatives' poll ratings sank to 24 per cent. This was as bad as the dark days of 1980–81, as the public did not believe economic recovery was happening, and Thatcher again fell back on making a virtue of her determined refusal to change policy. The autumn of 1985 brought no relief. In September and early October riots broke out again, not only in Brixton and Toxteth, but also in Tottenham and Handsworth. Soon after, a House of Lords select committee published a report warning of the irreparable loss of industrial capacity since 1979, and casting doubt on the government's claim that the expanding service sector would more than compensate. Once again Thatcher was compelled to declare at the party conference that dealing with unemployment was her top priority. But it kept rising, and at the end of 1985 the Church of England published a report, *Faith in the City*, deploring the demoralization and social breakdown in many urban areas.

In the course of that year a further issue arose that would cause increasing difficulties for Thatcher for the remainder of her prime ministership. As chancellor Lawson was a figure of considerable intellectual self-confidence; Thatcher was somewhat in awe of him, and never bullied or humiliated him as she had his predecessor, Howe. He initially shared her belief in the need to keep a tight rein on public spending and to bring inflation down, but he also had ideas of his own. Some of them concerned the reform and simplification of the tax system, and in the aftermath of the fall and recovery of sterling in January 1985, Lawson came to believe the United Kingdom should join the exchange rate mechanism (ERM) of the European monetary system, so as to prevent such destabilizing fluctuations in the currency markets in future. He was supported by Howe and Robin Leigh-Pemberton, the governor of the Bank of England, and in February 1985 Lawson and Howe put the case to Thatcher for joining the ERM, when the time was right; but she was unpersuaded. In November, when circumstances seemed more propitious, a larger group of ministers discussed the matter, and Whitelaw also came out in support. But Thatcher declared she would resign if Britain entered the ERM, since it would involve an unacceptable diminution of national sovereignty. For the next five years, she would resist all efforts by Lawson and Howe to change her mind, and this fundamental disagreement would eventually end their careers and her prime ministership.

Tainted victories

During the first two and a half years of her second term there were many signs that Thatcher's government seemed to have lost its way on the home front, and three particular episodes, from which she emerged victorious, also exposed her to much additional controversy and criticism. The first was the divisive and protracted dispute between the government and the coal miners. On taking office in 1979 Thatcher expected another confrontation with them, which she was determined to win: partly to avenge the defeat they had inflicted on Heath's government, and partly because her policy of taming the unions would be in ruins if she lost. But she was only prepared to take on the miners when she was ready, which was why she had shied away from doing battle with them in February 1981. Meanwhile, large stocks of coal were built up at many power stations, while others were converted to burn oil, making it possible for Thatcher to sit out a long strike. In March 1983 Lawson confirmed the appointment of Ian MacGregor, a hard-headed Scots-American businessman, as chairman of the National Coal Board with effect from September; and in the same year the government passed its third instalment of trade union reform, which made union leaders more accountable to their members by requiring secret ballots. By then the National Union of Mineworkers was led by the militant Arthur Scargill, who opposed all pit closures, even though the Coal Board was heading for a loss of £250 million in 1983–4; and he was determined to bring Thatcher down.

In the spring of 1984 the Coal Board announced the closure of twenty uneconomic pits, and Scargill called the miners out on a strike that would last for twelve months. There was solid support for him in Yorkshire, Scotland, and parts of south Wales; there was mass picketing of working pits, power stations, coal depots, and ports; and there were violent confrontations between the militant miners and the police which were regularly televised on news bulletins. But Scargill had refused to hold the ballot which the law now required, and many miners, especially in the Nottinghamshire coalfield, declined to join the strike. His disregard of the requisite democratic procedures, and his oft-expressed desire to overthrow the government, meant that neither the TUC nor the Labour Party would endorse his quasi-revolutionary objectives, and such sympathy as existed for the miners was outweighed by widespread revulsion at the picketing, intimidation, and ensuing violence. Thatcher implausibly insisted that the strike was an industrial dispute between management and workers in which the government declined to intervene, but she was on stronger ground in condemning Scargill's assault on freedom, democracy, and the rule of law. This was the greatest domestic crisis she faced, but after a bruising year Scargill was effectively defeated. By the end of October 1984 it was clear there was sufficient coal to last the winter, miners began to go back to the pits, and the following March their union delegates voted for a full return to work.

As well as crushing the external foe in the south Atlantic, Thatcher had now vanquished what she described as 'the enemy within';[14] but there were other people and organizations that she also wished to bring to heel. She had virtually grown up in the Grantham town council chamber, and the preservation of local government autonomy, as a counterpoise to the ever-extending reach of Whitehall, was a deeply ingrained Conservative belief. But municipal authorities no longer seemed to Thatcher what they had been in her father's day. Since the Second World War, she believed, they had become inefficient, extravagant, irresponsible, and often Labour-controlled, with the result that local government spending, like that of central government, had got out of control. These faults were especially marked in the recently created bodies that oversaw England's major conurbations: the GLC (set up by Wilson in 1965) and the six metropolitan counties of Merseyside, Greater Manchester, South Yorkshire, West Yorkshire, Tyne and Wear, and the West Midlands (established by Heath in 1974). The GLC was controlled by the provocatively left-wing Ken Livingstone ('Red Ken' to the Tory tabloids); the Liverpool corporation was dominated by the so-called Militant Tendency and led by Ted Knight ('Red Ted'); and David Blunkett was the chief commissar of the so-called 'People's Republic of South Yorkshire'. Thatcher was determined to emasculate these men and extinguish these municipalities.

In December 1983 the environment secretary, Patrick Jenkin, introduced a bill to give the government the power to cap the level of rates that any council might raise. It was denounced by Heath in the Commons, and met with serious opposition in the Lords, but it reached the statute book in June 1984, and Jenkin immediately imposed a cap on eighteen local authorities, of which sixteen were Labour-controlled. Most of them, including the GLC and Liverpool, tried to defy the government, by threatening not to set any budget for the following financial year; but they were forced to yield, not least because the Labour leader, Kinnock, disowned such practices. Next, in the autumn of 1984 the government introduced legislation to abolish the

GLC, having previously failed in its efforts to cancel the elections to it scheduled for the following year. Once again Heath led the opposition in the Commons, and the government's majority fell to twenty-three in the Lords; but the bill became law, and the GLC ceased to exist at the end of March 1986. Thatcher claimed that this resulted in an annual saving of £40 million, but the abolition of the GLC left one of the greatest cities in the world with no central authority responsible for strategic planning and infrastructural investment. In the same measure the six metropolitan counties were also abolished, and many of their functions were handed back to the old city corporations of Manchester, Liverpool, Leeds, Newcastle, Birmingham, and Sheffield.

Yet the greatest risk to Thatcher's position during her second term came neither from Arthur Scargill nor from her controversial local government reforms, but from a cabinet crisis that blew up late in 1985, for the unlikely reason that Westland plc, the United Kingdom's only maker of helicopters, was facing bankruptcy. Heseltine, the defence secretary, was determined it should be acquired by a continental consortium to ensure the continuing presence in Europe of a vital defence industry. But Brittan, whom Thatcher had recently demoted from the Home Office to the Department of Trade and Industry, supported the Westland shareholders, who preferred to sell to the American corporation Sikorski. He was backed by Thatcher, but Heseltine mounted an increasingly public campaign in favour of his alternative, European, option. By December 1985 Thatcher and Brittan were clear that Heseltine's scheme was dead; but, in defiance of the cabinet conventions of collective responsibility, he continued to pursue it, lobbying his business contacts to keep it alive. Thatcher failed to rein him in, and both sides began briefing against each other and leaking letters to the press. At a cabinet meeting on 9 January 1986 the Westland matter was raised again, and Heseltine stormed out and publicly announced his resignation. In the ensuing uproar Brittan failed to give a convincing response to accusations that he had been party to some of the leaked letters, and on 24 January he, too, resigned.

This was a shambles. Thatcher no longer seemed in command of her government, where cabinet responsibility had publicly broken down, and where she had failed to stop Heseltine pursuing his policy of seeking European support for Westland. She had been complicit in leaks and briefings by one of her own colleagues, namely Brittan, against another, Heseltine. Her refusal to publish a report on the affair by the cabinet secretary, Armstrong, further fuelled the suspicions that she was being less than candid, and that there was some sort of cover-up. And while there was little sympathy for Heseltine's theatrical resignation, there was a widespread feeling that she had let Brittan go so as to save her own skin. Thatcher's complicity in the leaks was known to some people in 10 Downing Street and at the Department of Trade and Industry, and Brittan could have ended her career had he publicly revealed all he knew about her involvement. But she survived the emergency Commons debate held at the end of January. Kinnock failed to ask precise and probing questions about what she knew and what she had done, and fell back on vague generalities. Thatcher replied in a carefully worded speech, admitting 'regret' at what had happened,[15] while Heseltine and Brittan both stayed their hands, and urged that it was time to move on.

None of these three victories enhanced Thatcher's reputation and nor did they improve the standing of her government. Although many believed Scargill had to be beaten, the protracted miners' strike, and the violence, bitterness, and recriminations that accompanied it, were not easily reconciled with Thatcher's wish to replace discord with harmony, and in many mining communities she would never be forgiven. The abolition of the GLC and the metropolitan counties seemed motivated more by partisan vindictiveness than by any serious attempt to make local government work better; it was an extraordinary assertion of centralizing power by a prime minister pledged to roll back the state; and while in the short run Ken Livingstone lost the battle for London, he would eventually win the war, being elected the city's first mayor in 2000. The Westland affair was even more damaging, casting doubt on Thatcher's command of her cabinet, and on the honesty and transparency she had so often proclaimed as being the essence of her politics and her personality. For the first time since 1982 there were mutterings in the Conservative Party about a leadership contest. Nothing came of them, and the Westland affair soon blew over; but during the early months of 1986 the Tories were still third in the opinion polls, and it would be from the back benches to which he had retired that Heseltine would eventually mount the challenge that would end Thatcher's premiership.

6

Thatcherism Triumphant? 1986–89

'The first seven years of Conservative government have produced some benefits for Britain . . . The next seven are going to produce more. . . . And the next seven after that, more still.'

(Margaret Thatcher, 1986)[1]

'In a year she'll be so unpopular you won't believe it.'

(Denis Thatcher to Carol Thatcher, 12 June 1987)[2]

Zenith

Although her second administration was buffeted by these political headwinds and cabinet cross-currents, it also witnessed the heyday of what was increasingly being described as 'Thatcherism', or 'popular capitalism'. In March 1986, two months after the Westland affair, Thatcher declared that tenants were 'jumping' at the opportunity to purchase their council houses, workers to buy shares in privatized companies, and trade unionists to exercise control over their leaders via the ballot.[3] The first of these claims was certainly correct. By September 1986 a million council houses had been sold and by the end of her premiership the number had reached one and a half million. As a result owner occupation grew from 55 per cent of the population in 1980 to 67 per cent ten years later, while local authority support for public sector housing significantly declined. For Thatcher, council estates were the seedbeds of socialism, vandalism, and crime, whereas home ownership was the defining virtue of good citizenship, and she successfully opposed all suggestions from Howe and Lawson that tax relief on mortgages should be phased out. Thatcher believed that increasing the number of home owners would help strangle socialism and embed Conservative values more deeply; moreover, by 1990 proceeds from council house sales had netted £28 billion for the Treasury.

This social revolution in home ownership was well under way by the beginning of Thatcher's second term; but it was only after 1983 that the privatization of state-owned corporations, many of them nationalized by Labour after 1945, became a major plank of government policy. The sale of shares in BT began in November 1984, and within eighteen months this raised almost £4 billion. Next came British Gas: as with BT, the shares were deliberately undervalued, they were many times oversubscribed, and prices rose spectacularly on the first day of trading. The third high-profile privatization was of British Airways; shares were eleven times oversubscribed, and prices rose by 82 per cent on the opening day. On the eve of the 1987 election Rolls-Royce was also returned to the private sector, thereby reversing Heath's controversial nationalization sixteen years before. Privatization was pragmatic and piecemeal, but it provided Thatcher with a defining purpose for her second administration: putting nationalization irrevocably into reverse, and enlarging the population of shareholders who had a stake in the capitalist system. She was eager to press further ahead (electricity and water would be earmarked for selling off in the next election manifesto), and by 1989 the proceeds of privatization amounted to £24 billion.

The successful sell-off of nationalized industries enabled Thatcher's second administration to regain some political momentum, as did the cumulative effect of the deregulation of restrictive practices carried on by management and unions alike, which helped to bring into being what was called the 'enterprise economy'. One reason Thatcher became so critical of universities and the Church of England was that academics and clerics seemed so hostile to business, which she (urged on by Denis) regarded as an essential activity and an admirable calling. During her second term she increasingly preached the gospel of wealth creation, and events and developments seemed to bear her out. Between 1983 and 1990 more than three million new jobs were generated, mostly in the service sector, which went some way towards making up for those that had earlier been lost in manufacturing, and by the end of her premiership more than 10 per cent of the workforce was self-employed. The most spectacular deregulation, which was the natural corollary to the earlier abolition of exchange controls, was the opening up of the City of London, known as the 'Big Bang', which took place in October 1986. Traditional gentlemanly practices of doing business were swept away; overseas banks, finance houses, and their employees were welcomed; and London was reinvented as a competitive international financial centre that could hold its own with Frankfurt, Tokyo, and New York—a reinvention vividly symbolized by the construction of new tall buildings in the old square mile and the regeneration of Docklands.

The transformative effect of these changes was undoubted, but they also had their downsides. In championing the sale of council houses Thatcher showed an intuitive understanding of the aspirations of many ordinary people; but the resulting decline in the stock of public housing, combined with soaring property prices later in the decade, meant there would be a significant shortage of affordable accommodation for many families on low incomes. Privatization made former nationalized industries more efficient and competitive, and was a policy that would subsequently be taken up in many other parts of the world; but it did not always end monopoly, the government used the proceeds as income to finance further tax cuts rather than to invest in long-overdue infrastructural repairs, and there was always the risk that the nation's essential utilities might end up in foreign ownership, as some indeed did. The creation of many new jobs in the service sector was undeniable, but it was largely confined to the south-east of the country, and the old manufacturing regions were devastated by de-industrialization: the closure of the factories, mills, steelworks, and mines on which the livelihoods of entire communities had depended. And while the 'Big Bang' rejuvenated the City, it also gave rise to what critics deplored as a materialistic culture of rampant greed, where speculation and a fast profit were more important than the creation of real wealth. It was a far cry from the spartan thrift and self-denial of Alfred Roberts.

All this helps explain why, between 1981 and 1987, average wages rose by 3 per cent a year. Hire-purchase restrictions had been lifted in 1982, and financial deregulation led to an unprecedented credit boom, as banks and building societies competed to offer ever easier loans; credit cards and cash-dispensers became widespread by the middle of the decade; and shops also stayed open for longer, so opportunities to spend also multiplied. Instead of being a nation of unionized producers, Britain was becoming, as Thatcher hoped it would, a nation of individualized consumers. But they were not, as Thatcher preached, good housekeepers, for the average British family was spending much more than it earned: indeed, personal indebtedness rose four times as fast between 1983 and 1987 as average incomes. Much of this borrowing financed home purchases, as average prices more than doubled between 1982 and 1989, and the number of mortgages doubled in 1986–7 alone. But while in the short run this credit spree and spending boom could be sustained, many people, including those who had bought their council houses, found that their homes were worth less than their mortgages when recession returned in the early 1990s. Moreover, unemployment went on rising until 1986, and a quarter of the population was living on less than half the national average income; but Thatcher did not seem to mind.

She was more concerned about the problem of domestic rates (the primary form of local government income), which she disliked as a tax that was only levied on property owners, and she was eager to find a way to prevent Labour councils from increasing charges on householders, many of whom voted Tory. Late in 1984 two junior ministers at the Department of the Environment, Kenneth Baker and William Waldegrave, began working on a proposal to replace rates by a scheme whereby everyone who used council services would pay towards the cost of them, whether they owned property or not. Thatcher became more fully engaged in the issue the following February, after protests in Scotland against the recent re-evaluation of the rates, and in May 1985 she told the Scottish Tory party conference that the rating system would be reformed, and that a new scheme would be first introduced north of the border where the grievances were strongest. Lawson warned Thatcher that the proposed reform would prove 'completely unworkable and politically catastrophic',[4] which was a prescient prediction. In January 1986 Baker, who had recently been promoted to be secretary of state for the environment, published a green paper, *Paying for Local Government*, which set out the detail of what was termed the 'community charge'. It received a mixed reception in the Commons and in the media, but by the end of the year the bill to abolish domestic rates in Scotland had been passed, and the community charge would come into full operation there on 1 April 1989.

The nation and the world

Although Thatcher was prime minister of the United Kingdom of Great Britain and Northern Ireland, she knew little about the manufacturing cities and industrial centres of the midlands and the north, and showed scant sympathy for their de-industrializing plight. Wales and Scotland were largely foreign countries to her, but as a committed unionist she was opposed to any calls for devolution. There was continuing bloodshed and violence in Northern Ireland, along with terrorist attacks in London, while the attempt to murder her at the Grand Hotel in Brighton in October 1984 only intensified her loathing of the IRA. Yet during her second term she came to recognize there must be a political solution to this unending carnage, and that view was shared by Garrett FitzGerald, who had become Irish taoiseach in December 1982, and also by the Irish lobby in Washington to which Reagan, whose forebears came from Tipperary, was sympathetic. In the aftermath of the Brighton bombing Thatcher's initial discussions with FitzGerald did not go well; but their personal relations were good, Reagan gently urged her to adopt a more accommodating attitude, and she began to understand that the law-abiding Catholic community in the north had to be reconciled to the British state.

The ensuing conversations were largely carried on, not by the Northern Ireland Office (where Douglas Hurd had replaced Prior late in 1984), but by the Cabinet Office, and the Ulster Unionists, who were opposed to any such conversations, were deliberately kept out. The eventual result was the Anglo-Irish agreement, which Thatcher and FitzGerald signed at Hillsborough Castle on 15 November 1985, which created a joint Anglo-Irish Intergovernmental Conference, thereby recognizing Dublin's involvement in any future peace process, and offering some reassurance to the Catholic population of Ulster. As over Rhodesia, Thatcher had to be nudged and encouraged, this time especially by the cabinet secretary, Armstrong, in a direction she was not wholly comfortable in going, and her doubts were borne out by the outraged reaction of the Ulster Unionists to what they regarded as a British betrayal. Nor did the violence and killing in Northern Ireland abate thereafter, and the agreement failed to deliver the cross-border co-operation against terrorism for which Thatcher had hoped. But opinion in the republic and in Britain was generally in favour; the agreement did help convince the Americans that Britain was genuinely trying to resolve the Northern Ireland problem; and it was the tentative beginning of a process which would end with the Good Friday agreement of 1998.

Having held on to the Falklands and let go of Rhodesia during her first term, Thatcher was now faced with another late imperial challenge in the form of Hong Kong, the United Kingdom's last great colony, on which the lease was due to expire in 1997, when it would revert to China. Much as she would have liked to deliver another Falklands-like triumph in the Far East, this was impossible both militarily and legally, as the Chinese leader Deng Xiaoping had made brutally plain to her when she had visited him in Beijing in September 1982. Britain's best hope was to try to ensure that the colony's capitalist way of life would be preserved following the unavoidable advent of Chinese rule. Thatcher recognized these would be the best terms she could get for the Hong Kong people, and Howe eventually secured an agreement in September 1984 whereby the Chinese government, which in fact had no wish to destroy Hong Kong's prosperity, guaranteed its 'special status', once they had repossessed it, for fifty years. In December, Thatcher flew to Beijing to sign the agreement, and then went on to reassure the people of Hong Kong that this was a good deal. The suppression of dissidents in Tiananmen Square, Beijing, in June 1989 would severely shake her confidence in the Chinese government's *bona fides*; but the settlement was the best that could realistically have been hoped for, and she would attend the final handover in 1997.

Once again Thatcher had acquiesced in a 'pragmatic' solution which went against her combative and confrontational instincts that were as marked in overseas as in domestic affairs. But in the case of South Africa, which was a British and Commonwealth issue, she was more defiant and determined, for she consistently opposed the widely held view that economic sanctions were the necessary means to end white minority rule, and she seemed to relish the isolation and opprobrium she endured as a result. The fact that such opinions were held by many Commonwealth and European leaders merely strengthened her conviction that she was right. For Thatcher saw the issue of apartheid in cold war rather than post-colonial terms: white South Africa was part of the West, whereas the African National Congress (ANC) was at best a communist-backed, and at worst a terrorist, organization. If the ANC was allowed to prevail, Thatcher believed, the South African economy would be destroyed, and a government would be installed that would be more sympathetic to Moscow than to Washington. Imposing economic sanctions would make this outcome more likely, not less; whereas increasing trade with South Africa, instead of reducing it, would open up the nation to the outside world, strengthen its economy still further, and improve the chances of a peaceful transition to black majority rule, which she reluctantly recognized must eventually come.

Although Thatcher's view of South African affairs possessed a certain internal logic, she made two serious misjudgements. In standing out against the rest of the Commonwealth she was also setting herself against the Queen, who cared far more for it than Thatcher ever did. Moreover, in denouncing the ANC as a communist and terrorist organization, she failed to recognize that other members shared Nelson Mandela's strong commitment to democracy and the rule of law. Instead, she was determined to block the imposition of further sanctions. In September 1985 she vetoed such a proposal by the EC, and the following month, at the Commonwealth heads of government meeting in Nassau, she was equally unyielding, although she had no supporters from any other member country, and Howe found her intransigence embarrassing. At a meeting held in London twelve months later, the Commonwealth leaders overrode British dissent and agreed to implement the sanctions package proposed at Nassau. Britain, Howe lamented, was branded as the 'sole defender' of apartheid.[5] Thatcher had hoped that by fending off further punitive measures she would be able to persuade South Africa's prime minister, P. W. Botha, to embrace reform voluntarily. But he was as uncompromising as she was.

Thatcher's relations with Commonwealth leaders deteriorated during her second term, but those with the EC for a time improved—or at least seemed to do so. In June 1984 she achieved a permanent budget settlement at Fontainebleau (the deal Carrington and Gilmour had negotiated in 1981 was about to expire), grudgingly agreed to by Helmut Kohl and Mitterrand so as to keep her quiet; but it was less of a triumphant deal than she claimed. The following year she supported the appointment of Jacques Delors as president of the European Commission, and backed the Single European Act (1986), furthering the original commitments enshrined in the treaty of Rome to the free movement of goods, services, capital, and people; but she would later regret it, because it extended the powers of the commission and the Strasbourg parliament, and was a significant step in the direction of that greater integration which she deplored. The high point of Thatcher's enthusiasm for Europe was her agreement with Mitterrand, announced in January 1986, that Britain and France would collaborate in constructing a Channel tunnel to link London and Paris by rail. It was the sort of practical project she found more appealing than the visionary schemes for a united Europe that, to her dismay, Delors would soon embrace, but she would not mention it when she came to write her memoirs.

As during her first term, Thatcher's most significant overseas preoccupations were Britain's relations with the United States and the continuing cold war. The conclusion she drew from Reagan's belated support over the Falklands, and his failure to consult her over Grenada, was that she must get even closer to him. She was also looking for a younger Soviet leader who might replace the ailing Politburo gerontocracy (Andropov died in 1984, and his successor, Konstantin Chernenko, lasted barely a year), and she discovered him in Mikhail Gorbachev, whom she invited to Chequers in December 1984. She found him open-minded and prepared to argue; promptly declared she could 'do business' with him;[6] and advised Reagan to do the same, which he did, once Gorbachev took over on Chernenko's death. But these decisions and developments carried their own risks. In April 1986 Thatcher allowed the use of British-based American F111s to bomb Libya, in retaliation for attacks on US servicemen and tourists in Europe. There was widespread opposition in Britain, even as Thatcher was determined to show herself Reagan's staunchest ally. And when Reagan met Gorbachev in Reykjavik six months later, he was so convinced that the Strategic Defense Initiative (known as 'Star Wars') would render the United States invulnerable to Soviet missile attack that he offered to cut America's strategic nuclear weapons by half in five years, and to eliminate them entirely in a decade. Thatcher was horrified, for Reagan was ignoring Britain's independent deterrent, and showing himself more of a unilateralist than Foot or the CND.

'Ten More Years'?

For most of its second term Thatcher's government fared poorly in the polls. The defeat of Scargill did not give her the lift that the victory over Galtieri had earlier provided; unemployment remained high, and economic recovery was slow and uneven; the Westland crisis had weakened her moral and political authority; and her relations with Reagan continued to be more tense in private than she let on in public. But by the autumn of 1986 the polls began to improve for the Tories, as the policies pursued by Howe and Lawson finally began to produce results. In his March budget Lawson had cut the basic rate of income tax by one penny to twenty-nine pence in the pound, and towards the end of the year unemployment began to fall for the first time since Thatcher took power. Moreover, low inflation and low interest rates combined to make Britain one of the fastest-growing economies in the EC, and in the aftermath of the Big Bang the City of London was beginning to thrive. There was talk of a 'British economic miracle', but the so-called 'Lawson boom' was both partial and fragile, for it depended on a consumer surge driven by increasing household indebtedness, and on using the income derived from North Sea oil and privatization to finance tax cuts. In 1986 industrial investment was still lower than it had been when Thatcher became prime minister, and the following year Britain's gross national product fell behind that of Italy.

Nevertheless, the beginnings of the 'Lawson boom' and the apparent success of 'popular capitalism' meant that the Tory party conference in October 1986 was more upbeat than its recent predecessors, as ministers promised further privatization and increased spending on hospitals and the police. Thatcher insisted that the Conservatives were the caring party, exulted that privatization was being taken up around the world, and denounced Labour's commitment to a non-nuclear defence policy and the closure of American bases in Britain as irresponsible and unpatriotic. By the end of the year the Tories had consolidated their lead in the polls, and they maintained and hardened it through to the following spring. In March 1987 Lawson produced a vote-winning budget, cutting the standard rate of income tax by a further two pence, while also increasing spending on health and other services. Soon after, Thatcher paid a triumphant visit to Moscow, to do more 'business' with Gorbachev during seven hours of formal talks: on British television she appeared a world leader of unrivalled stature, as welcome and influential in the Kremlin as she was in the White House. This was high-level summitry, but it was also deliberate pre-electioneering, and soon after her return, she announced that the poll would be held on 11 June.

Yet the Conservative electoral campaign was less confident and coherent in 1987 than it had been four years earlier. The manifesto was poorly written, and although full of policy proposals, in an effort to be more specific than its predecessor, many of them had not been thought through. Thatcher had also come to distrust Tebbit, whom she had moved from trade and industry to be party chairman in September 1985, and she intruded Lord Young into Conservative central office, but the result was a divided and often ill-focused Tory campaign, beset by personal rivalries and animosities, whereas Labour's effort, overseen by Peter Mandelson and Bryan Gould, was a great improvement on its predecessor. Some in central office thought Thatcher had become a liability, because her campaigning style, like her prime ministerial manner, was increasingly hectoring and overbearing, and they argued that she should play a less prominent part than in 1983. She also made some unexpected gaffes at press conferences and in interviews, and when a poll published a week before the election suggested that Labour was closing the gap, she panicked and became convinced that everything was going wrong. There was a succession of blazing rows at central office which led Whitelaw to conclude, presciently, that 'that is a woman who will never fight another election'.[7]

During the campaign's final days Thatcher recovered her nerve and composure, and the Tories commandingly outspent their opponents on last-minute advertising. The voters still did not trust Labour on defence or the economy, while the Liberal–SDP Alliance failed to become the second party in the state, but was still popular enough to split the opposition vote. As a result Thatcher won by another landslide, even though it was not quite on the scale of 1983, as the Tories did badly in Scotland, Wales, and the north of England, and drew most of their support from the shires, the suburbs, and the south-east of England. They lost twenty-one seats, while Labour gained twenty, and the Alliance won a mere twenty-two. Labour's share of the vote increased from 27.6 to 30.8 per cent, and the Tory share declined slightly, from 42.4 to 42.2 per cent, while the Alliance only obtained 22.6 per cent. As in 1983 Thatcher easily held Finchley (though her majority was reduced slightly, to 8,913), and her ambition to retain her three-figure Commons preponderance was just realized, even as it was reduced from 144 seats to 102. Although the Conservatives had won three successive general elections between 1951 and 1959 they had done so with three different leaders; no one *man* had achieved so many victories since before the Great Reform Act of 1832, and for a *woman* to have done so was even more remarkable.

Thatcher had been compelled to reshuffle her 1983 cabinet several times in the aftermath of such events as Parkinson's enforced resignation and the Westland affair, and following the election she reshaped it again. Howe stayed at the Foreign Office, Lawson at the Treasury, and Hurd at the Home Office (where she had moved him in September 1985 from Northern Ireland), while Whitelaw continued as deputy prime minister and leader of the Lords. Hailsham retired as lord chancellor, and was followed briefly by Lord Havers and at greater length by Lord Mackay of Clashfern. Parkinson returned to the cabinet as secretary of state for energy, while Walker, the previous holder of that office, was moved to be Welsh secretary. Yet this was scarcely a 'Thatcherite' government, and many of its members were 'up and coming pragmatists from the centre-left of the party',[8] among them Kenneth Baker, Kenneth Clarke, Norman Fowler, Tom King, and John Major, who entered the cabinet for the first time as chief secretary to the Treasury. Joseph, her mentor and most loyal supporter, had already retired from the cabinet in May 1986, having fallen foul of the teachers' unions in his drive for educational reform. Tebbit, once one of her key supporters, had become so disenchanted with Thatcher that he decided to leave the government, though he also did so to care for his wife, who had been permanently disabled as a result of the IRA bombing of the Grand Hotel. More damaging would be the retirement of Whitelaw in January 1988 on health grounds: he had been utterly loyal to Thatcher, but also gave candid advice as to what she should or shouldn't do. He was irreplaceable, and his departure left the prime minister increasingly isolated.

But, compared with the indecisiveness that the Thatcher government had displayed in the immediate aftermath of the 1983 electoral triumph, the early months of her third term represented a much more active and purposeful beginning. Thatcher herself chaired an inter-departmental committee which in March 1988 pledged £3 billion in aid for the inner cities. There was a further phase of privatization, beginning with British Petroleum, which would be followed by the sale of the nine existing water authorities and of the twelve regional electricity distribution companies. At education, where he proved a more emollient and effective minister than Joseph had been, Baker passed legislation setting up a national curriculum, giving schools the right to opt out of local authority control, and abolishing the inner London education authority. At health, Clarke empowered hospitals to become self-governing 'NHS trusts' within the health service, funded by the taxpayer but with control of their own budgets. And between December 1987 and July 1988 Thatcher drove through the legislation which would introduce the community charge in England and Wales, which became known as the 'poll tax' (since it was levied on individuals not properties, and made no distinction between rich and poor), despite the opposition of Heath, Heseltine, and Gilmour in the Commons, and even more strenuous and protracted hostility in the Lords.

By launching such a veritable frenzy of legislation and new initiatives Thatcher was determined to prove there would be no slowing down during her third term, and that she might just go 'on, and on, and on'.[9] The Conservative Party conference in the autumn of 1987 was an unabashed victory rally, with no equivalent of the Parkinson revelations that had marred the proceedings in 1983, and Thatcher immodestly hinted at her intention of beating Lord Liverpool's record of fifteen continuous years in office. Until early 1989 the government's poll ratings held up much better than they had during the first two years of her first and second terms; and on 3 May 1989 Thatcher completed ten years in power, making her the longest serving prime minister of the twentieth century, surpassing Asquith's continuous term and Churchill's two separate stints at 10 Downing Street. Her comment was suitably regal: 'we feel quite a sense of achievement that we have completed ten years . . . during that time, Britain has been transformed'.[10] And at the party conference that autumn the Tory faithful, to whom she seemed indomitable, invincible, infallible, and indispensable, gave her a rapturous reception, chanting 'Ten more years, ten more years'.[11] Yet within little more than twelve months, she would be gone.

7

Isolation and Defenestration, 1989–90

'I am still at the crease, though the bowling has been pretty hostile of late.'

(Margaret Thatcher, 12 November 1990)[1]

'I had lost the Cabinet's support. I could not even muster a credible campaign team. It was the end.'

(Margaret Thatcher, 1993)[2]

Injury time

After a decade in power it was increasingly clear who were Thatcher's friends, and who were her enemies. At the 1987 election the press had supported her government by a margin of three to one: *The Daily Mirror*, *The Guardian*, and *The Independent* were left of centre, but *The Times*, *The Daily Telegraph*, *The Express*, *The Daily Mail* (and their Sunday siblings), *The Sun*, and the *News of the World* were strongly Thatcherite. In 1981 Rupert Murdoch had acquired *The Times* and the *Sunday Times*, despite his already extensive share of the newspaper market. Thatcher always denied any involvement in these transactions, but in fact she had met with Murdoch early in the year, something she later and consistently refused to acknowledge. In October 1990 Sky TV was allowed to take over its only rival, British Satellite Broadcasting, again without reference to the Monopolies Commission. Throughout her years in power Thatcher helped Murdoch expand his media interests, and backed him in his battles with the print unions (notably during the Wapping dispute of 1986–7), and he was a loyal supporter in return. She bestowed knighthoods on well-disposed editors, such as David English of *The Daily Mail* and Albert (Larry) Lamb of *The Sun*. She gave peerages to favoured businessmen such as John King (British Airways), Arnold Weinstock (GEC), Victor Matthews (Trafalgar House), and Jeffrey Sterling (P&O). And, when making public appointments, she sought to put in like-minded people, as when she replaced Gordon Richardson, the governor of the Bank of England who did not share her belief in monetarism, with Robin Leigh-Pemberton, who did: 'is he one of us?', she was reputed to have asked each time she was presented with a suggestion for appointment.[3]

On the other side of the political divide were those organizations that were not of Thatcher's 'way of thinking', such as the universities, the arts establishment, the Church of England, and the BBC. There, also, she determined to put in her own people, to bring these wayward cultures to heel, as at the BBC, where she appointed Marmaduke Hussey, the former managing director of Times Newspapers, to be chairman of the governors; his first act was to sack Alasdair Milne, the widely respected director-general. Yet the greatest threat to Thatcher's position did not come from her political opponents, but from those who claimed to be on the same side. She would always be the darling of the Tory party conferences, but while she had purged the 'wets' from her cabinet, they had not gone away, and as her tenure at Downing Street lengthened, she made new enemies in her own party. During the eleven years that she held office thirty-six cabinet ministers departed, and several of them, such as Gilmour and Heseltine, became fierce critics. Many ministers resented the way that Bernard Ingham would brief the press against them, and by her third term the cabinet was no longer the place where decisions were taken, but merely where they were reported. At the same time Thatcher was increasingly out of touch with her back-benchers: those who had been in parliament a long time were resentful that she had not given them jobs, while she scarcely knew any of those who had arrived in 1987.

It was the same in the country as a whole, where Thatcher was a self-styled populist premier who was never all that popular: although she obtained two overwhelming Commons majorities, most of the votes in 1983 and again four years later were cast against her. There were also many who lost out during the 1980s; the boom times in the City and the south-east, along with de-industrialization and high unemployment elsewhere, meant that inequality markedly increased. Between 1979 and 1992 average household incomes rose by 36 per cent: but while those of the top 10 per cent went up by 62 per cent, those of the bottom 10 per cent fell by 17 per cent. The poll tax only made matters worse, since it was levied in such a way that thrifty, prudent home owners, many of whom had recently bought their council houses, were worse off, whereas those with high incomes were often better off. When it came into force in Scotland in April 1989 there was widespread refusal to pay. The following year it was introduced in England and Wales, where the opposition was even more pronounced. In March 1990 there were protests in Manchester, Bristol, and Birmingham, and several London boroughs, and there was a massive demonstration in Trafalgar Square which turned ugly, with rioting and looting. Thatcher came to regard commitment to the poll tax as the ultimate test of personal loyalty, but it was widely seen as an avoidable and unnecessary fiasco for which she was personally responsible.

It was against this darkening political and economic background that Lawson delivered his first post-election budget in April 1988, embodying and proclaiming the 'bourgeois triumphalism' that erstwhile supporters had come to deplore in the aftermath of Thatcher's third election victory. He cut the standard rate of income tax again from twenty-seven to twenty-five pence in the pound, while slashing the top rate from 60 to 40 per cent. This was another budget which blatantly favoured the rich, and since it coincided with cuts in unemployment benefit, housing benefit, and child benefit, it intensified the view that the Thatcher government was indifferent to increasing inequality. Moreover, the chancellor's give-away bonanza was fatally mistimed, for it merely stoked the 'Lawson boom', largely based on rising house prices and expanded consumer credit, which was getting out of control. By the end of 1989 inflation was back to 10 per cent, which was what it had been ten years earlier; interest rates had been pushed up to 15 per cent; and unemployment, while it had recently fallen, was still at two million. The combined effect of renewed inflation and increased interest rates hit the new, Thatcherite middle class—of self-employed businessmen, and owners of recently purchased homes—particularly hard.

Thatcher had been worried that the economy was overheating since the autumn of 1986, and there was another subject on which she increasingly came to disagree with her chancellor. For Lawson, like Howe, was in favour of joining the ERM, a policy to which the premier was viscerally hostile from 1985 to 1990. But it was widely understood that one day Britain would indeed join, and Lawson began to prepare the ground by trying to align sterling with the Deutschmark. Thatcher was flatly opposed to this policy, and to strengthen her hand in dealing with Lawson she brought back Alan Walters, who had worked for her between 1981 and 1983, to be her economic adviser. To complicate matters still further she was becoming increasingly antagonistic to the EC and to Jacques Delors; and in this view she was reinforced by Charles Powell, who had been her private secretary for international affairs since 1984, but who was by this time widely regarded as her *de facto* foreign secretary. His hand was much in evidence in the speech Thatcher delivered at Bruges in September 1988, where she said many complimentary things about Britain's destiny being in Europe, but the most memorable sentence gave a very different message: 'We have not successfully rolled back the frontiers of the state in Britain, only to see them re-imposed at a European level with a European super-state exercising a new dominance from Brussels'.[4] To Howe and Lawson alike, these views were anathema.

The long-festering disagreement between Howe and Lawson on the one hand, and Thatcher on the other, finally erupted in June 1989, at the European Council meeting in Madrid. They both urged that she should undertake to join the ERM by the end of 1992. She refused to follow their advice, on the grounds that the time was not right, which effectively left her isolated. She thought that Howe and Lawson had backed her into a corner, and in July she took out her rage and frustration by sacking Howe from the Foreign Office (where she replaced him with Major), and making him leader of the Commons instead. Although she gave him the title of deputy prime minister, the demotion of Howe was widely regarded as vindictive and ungrateful, and the ensuing cabinet reshuffle was not well received. Nor was Lawson happy, since the advice Thatcher was getting from Walters merely reinforced her determination not to join the ERM. By the autumn of 1989 Lawson had had enough, and he resigned in late October (making Walters's position untenable; he also quit a few days later). Thatcher moved Major back from the Foreign Office to replace Lawson, and translated Hurd from the Home Office to the Foreign Office. Ironically it was Major and Hurd who prevailed where Howe and Lawson had failed, for in October 1990 Thatcher finally agreed that Britain should indeed join the ERM.

The quarrels between Thatcher, Howe, and Lawson over Europe, combined with the poll tax débâcle and the return of inflation and high interest rates, increasingly gave the impression that the government was losing its way. Having held up unexpectedly well in the polls since June 1987, public opinion turned sharply and decisively against Thatcher and her colleagues early in 1989. That summer the Conservatives suffered their first national defeat under her leadership, when Labour won forty-five seats to the Tories' thirty-two in the elections to the European parliament. Labour also moved ahead in the opinion polls, where it would remain for the rest of Thatcher's premiership. In November 1989 Sir Anthony Meyer, an obscure Europhile Tory back-bencher, challenged Thatcher for the party leadership. She won by 314 votes to his 33 (with a further three abstentions and 24 spoilt papers); but the very fact there was a contest was more disturbing than comforting. By late 1989 Labour was heading towards a 50 per cent approval level; by February 1990 it was regarded as the party most likely to win the next election; and by the spring, Thatcher's personal rating had plummeted to 20 per cent, worse than in 1981. Her cabinet colleagues were finding her increasingly impossible to work with, while many Tory MPs were coming to believe that the best way to preserve the Thatcher legacy, and to keep their own seats, might be to get rid of Thatcher herself.

Global wobbles

By the time of her third election victory Thatcher was the unrivalled senior figure on the international stage, at least in terms of personality, if not of power. She had often been more pragmatic in foreign affairs than she let on, and had generally fared better when she adopted that approach. She had been intransigent over the Falklands, to her great benefit; but over Europe she became increasingly belligerent, with less obviously successful results, and having grudgingly given way over joining the ERM, it was at the wrong time and the wrong rate. She constantly stressed her close relationship with Reagan, but although the chemistry was good, and she could always overwhelm him in argument, she was more the junior partner than she would ever publicly acknowledge, and their disagreements, over the Falklands, Grenada, and 'Star Wars', had been deep. And while Thatcher had been the first western leader to recognize Gorbachev's significance, and liked to present herself as a latter-day Churchill, brokering high-level conversations between Washington and Moscow, the reality was that once Reagan and Gorbachev had begun to talk to each other, they no longer needed her as their intermediary.

Reagan's second term had only a year and a half to run when Thatcher secured her third electoral victory, and for much of it he was mired in the Iran–Contra scandal. By this time, under pressure from members of his own administration, he had backed off from his belief in the 'Star Wars' deterrent and thus from unilateral nuclear disarmament, much to Thatcher's relief. Within the limits of diplomatic politesse he had done all he could to express support for Thatcher's re-election, including humiliating the Labour leader, Kinnock, on his visit to Washington in March 1987, when he had been allowed barely twenty minutes in the Oval Office. Soon after her victory Thatcher returned to Washington, and gave Reagan a ringing endorsement when he was low in spirits and in the polls. In June 1988 he made a farewell visit to Thatcher in London, when each paid the other extravagant public tributes. In November that year she was his last official visitor to the White House, when she saluted the outgoing president, and tried to establish closer links with his successor, George H. W. Bush, who had been Reagan's vice-president. But the chemistry between them did not work so well. Sensitive to accusations of wimpishness in the election campaign, and being by American standards a well-born son of privilege, Bush was determined not to be intimidated or patronized by Thatcher as Reagan had often been.

This American distancing from Thatcher became apparent in the aftermath of the fall of the Berlin Wall and the collapse of communism in the autumn of 1989. Thatcher took pride and pleasure in claiming that this further extension of freedom was what she and Reagan had worked for; but that was only one of the reasons why communism foundered, and by no means the most important; and ironically, for someone who so welcomed this development, the consequences were in many ways not to her liking. She was determined to thwart the reunification of Germany, which she (mistakenly) regarded as portending a return to 1939 yet (rightly) feared would diminish British influence on both sides of the Atlantic. But Bush was equally determined that reunification would happen, and working with Kohl and Mitterrand, and eventually with Gorbachev, he largely ignored and increasingly isolated Thatcher, and helped bring about an outcome which she was powerless to prevent. As a result the future American route into Europe would be more via Berlin than via London. While the cold war had persisted Britain had enjoyed privileged access to

Washington, as America's essential continental partner, which Thatcher had exploited to the full; but once it was over the US–UK 'special relationship' would never be as close again, and a reunified Germany would be re-established as the major European power, not just economically, but politically and internationally too.

The collapse of communism almost coincided with the beginning of the end of apartheid in South Africa. There, too, Thatcher aspired to be a peace broker, but this was an implausible ambition, given her intransigence over sanctions and her continued hostility to the ANC. In 1989 the equally stubborn President Botha was replaced by the more accommodating F. W. de Klerk, and Thatcher pressed him to begin releasing African political prisoners and to negotiate a settlement that would bring in black majority rule; but at the Commonwealth heads of government meeting at Kuala Lumpur in October 1989 there was another row over sanctions, as Thatcher publicly repudiated the very agreement whose adoption she had proposed. Meanwhile, de Klerk gradually began to release the prisoners; early in 1990 all those who remained were freed, including Mandela, and the ban on political organizations such as the ANC was lifted. Thatcher and Mandela finally met in London in July: she was impressed by his dignity and lack of bitterness, but still feared he was a Marxist; he found her formidable but unyielding on the subject of sanctions and suspicious of the ANC. After her fall she would grudgingly concede that the only possible rulers of a post-apartheid South Africa would be Mandela and the ANC; but it was not the outcome she had wanted, and she was never wholly comfortable with it.

During her final months in power the invasion of Kuwait by Saddam Hussein in August 1990 provided further evidence of Thatcher's declining influence in world (and especially Anglo-American) affairs. The news broke when she was in the United States, attending the fortieth anniversary conference of the Aspen Institute in Colorado, so she had ample opportunity to urge that President Bush should stand firm, and later claimed much credit for his having done so. But even as she once again denounced dictatorial aggression, this was not as straightforward a war for Thatcher as winning back the Falklands had been, for Kuwait was an independent nation, not a British colony; and throughout the 1980s the United Kingdom had been supplying arms to Iraq to assist Saddam in his fight with Iran. Moreover, Bush needed no stiffening from Thatcher. It was he, not she, who was the Western leader, in charge of putting together the international coalition that would expel Saddam from Kuwait; and in the subsequent military campaign the United States was overwhelmingly the dominant partner, while Britain played a very subordinate part. In any case, by the time Kuwait was liberated Thatcher was no longer in Downing Street.

Endgame

By the early autumn of 1990 the signals for Thatcher were far from encouraging, both domestically and internationally, although it was unclear whether she noticed or even cared. In the aftermath of her Bruges speech, relations with most of her cabinet colleagues were more tense and vexed than ever; the Tory party was becoming increasingly divided over Europe; the poll tax had been a disaster; and the 'Lawson boom' seemed out of control. Stagflation was returning, and 1990 increasingly seemed like 1979 all over again, which cast serious doubt on Thatcher's claim that the pain endured by many people and places in the intervening years had been worth it. She had also lost out over the reunification of Germany, and her influence both in Washington and in Europe was seriously declining. At home and overseas she was increasingly isolated and embattled; but she gave no sign of it in her confident speech to the party conference in October 1990, where she took all the credit she could for the fall of communism, vowed never to appease Saddam, insisted that Britain would not join the single European currency, and scorned and ridiculed Labour. Once again the party faithful demanded 'Ten more years'. But on 2 November, Howe resigned.

His ostensible reason was Thatcher's response to the late October meeting of the European Council in Rome, where there had been a push to establish a single European currency by 2000, which she vehemently opposed. When reporting back to the Commons, her prepared statement had passed off without incident, but in answer to a subsequent question, she rejected Delors's plans for a more consolidated continent with the words 'No. No. No'.[5] Howe, who by this time was the only surviving member of her original 1979 cabinet apart from Thatcher herself, thereupon quit, declaring it was impossible for Britain to retain a position of influence in European affairs when she was so intransigent. He made his case with far greater force in the Commons, stressing that the United Kingdom should have joined the ERM much earlier, and ridiculing Thatcher's 'nightmare image' of a European super-state. It was, he concluded, no longer possible to reconcile his 'instinct of loyalty' to the prime minister with the 'true interests' of Britain.[6] It was a devastating performance, and all the more so coming from a mild-mannered and long-suffering minister, who was taking his belated revenge for the decade of bullying and humiliation he had endured at Thatcher's hands.

Heseltine had been biding his time since his dramatic resignation in 1986, and he now seized his opportunity, challenging Thatcher for the Tory leadership, in a contest she was confident she would win. But her campaign team, led by George Younger, lacked focus, co-ordination, and drive; many back-benchers had had scarcely any dealings with her; and those with marginal seats feared they would lose them if she led the party into the next election. She would again be let down by poor staff work, and made matters worse by departing to Paris on the eve of the ballot, to a meeting of the Commission on Security and Co-operation in Europe, attended by Bush, Gorbachev, Kohl, and Mitterrand. It was a celebration of the end of the cold war, and Thatcher wanted to claim her share of the credit, but her decision to go made her seem even more remote from her MPs. In the first ballot, held on 20 November, she won 204 votes to Heseltine's 152 (with 16 abstentions), which was four short of the margin required. She returned to London determined to fight on, but soon realized her support was ebbing away. She consulted her cabinet colleagues individually, most of whom told her that, having failed to secure the requisite votes on the first ballot, she could not win on the second. The next morning, 22 November, Thatcher announced her withdrawal from the contest, only staying on as prime minister until the party elected her successor as leader.

Having grudgingly agreed to resign, Thatcher produced a final bravura parliamentary performance later the same day, replying to a Labour no-confidence motion which was rendered pointless by her impending departure. Facing down her enemies on both sides of the house, she defended her record, demolished all interruptions, and restated the case that both domestically and internationally she had halted and reversed Britain's decline. It was an extraordinary display of parliamentary courage and command, and led many Tories to wonder how the party could have been so misguided as to ditch their most successful leader of modern times. But they had done the right thing, for while Thatcher would always retain some loyal supporters she had stayed too long, and the cabinet, the Commons, and the country had had enough—of the bullying and berating, the hectoring and handbagging. Just as she had been elected leader because she was not Heath, so Major, who succeeded her on 28 November, became leader because he was not Thatcher. Indeed, the two most memorable phrases of his campaign were scarcely veiled criticisms of his predecessor's excesses: the idea of a 'classless society' signalled a different view of the growing inequality that Thatcher had not merely tolerated but also justified, while a 'nation at ease with itself' offered an alternative vision to the ten unrelenting years of conflict and confrontation that had gone before.

8

Aftermath and Afterlife, 1990–2013

'I had passed from the well-lit world of public life, where I had lived so long, into . . . what? . . . I would have gone mad without work.'

(Margaret Thatcher, 1995)[1]

'Oh for an hour of the Iron Lady – although admittedly she went mad at the end.'

(Lord Dacre to Hugh Lloyd-Jones, 6 November 1997)[2]

Discontented retirement

Thatcher left 10 Downing Street on 28 November 1990, and having taken her farewell of the Queen she departed with Denis for the home in Dulwich they had purchased in 1986. It was too far from central London, and they soon moved to a large town house, 73 Chester Square, in Belgravia. But finding the right place to live was the least of Thatcher's post-prime ministerial problems. She never came to terms with her brutal defenestration, which was the same fate, magnified many times over, that her father had suffered when he had been unceremoniously ejected from Grantham town council, and for the rest of her life she would be bitter and resentful about it. According to one close aide, 'she never had a happy day after being ousted from office'.[3] All of her adult life she had lived for work, for politics, and for power; but she was now down and out, and there was no possibility of another high-level job, because she had offended too many people and was rightly regarded as an impossible colleague. Until her health gave way she spent much of her time travelling the world, giving lucrative speeches to the faithful who still turned out to cheer her, especially in the United States, but also in Japan and the Far East. Denis had always been reasonably well-off, her lectures were well paid, and Major immediately awarded all former prime ministers an additional annual allowance.

Thatcher was, as she conceded, 'comfortable' in retirement, but she was never contented. Her largest immediate task at least made her yet more comfortable, as Murdoch's Harper-Collins paid £3.5 million for her memoirs, which appeared in two volumes in 1993 and 1995. She wrote little of them herself, but took the project very seriously, and the books bear the strong imprint of her intimidating personality. She was concerned to secure her reputation, and this was the more urgent because her former colleagues were publishing their own versions of events, some of which were highly critical, among them Heseltine (*Where There's a Will*, 1987), Gilmour (*Dancing with Dogma*, 1992), Lawson (*The View from No. 11*, 1992), and Howe (*Conflict of Loyalty*, 1994). The first volume to appear was *The Downing Street Years*, in which Thatcher offered a highly tendentious account of Britain's 'decline', likened herself to the earl of Chatham in believing that she alone could save the country, and then described how she believed she had done so. Like Thatcher herself the book was devoid of humour, and was conspicuously lacking in magnanimity, since she described everyone who disagreed with her as a knave or a fool or an incompetent. It sold well, but the second volume, *The Path to Power*, in which she implausibly claimed she had always been a Thatcherite, even under Heath, and offered some controversial comments on international developments since she had left office, aroused less interest.

Thatcher sought to secure her legacy in other ways, one of which was by donating her massive archive to Churchill College, Cambridge: this was a deliberate snub to Oxford, whose failure to award her an honorary degree still rankled, and it also meant her papers would be 'with Winston's'. But she relented slightly when it came to issuing a CD-ROM of her complete public statements, which was produced by Oxford University Press in 1998. She also set up the Thatcher Foundation to promote her ideas around the world, which established offices in London, Washington, and Warsaw. But the money did not come in as she had hoped; the high-profile, high-impact role she had envisaged for it never came off; and it gradually evolved into a more modest educational philanthropy. One reason the funds did not flow was that Mark Thatcher told too many potential donors who had done well during the 1980s that it was 'payback time'.[4] His own business affairs, in which he traded shamelessly on his mother's name, continued to attract controversy and investigation from the tax authorities, and in 1996 he relocated to South Africa. Carol, meanwhile, continued her career as a jobbing journalist, but she, too, exploited her name by publishing an affectionate biography of her father in 1996, which was also highly critical of her mother.

For someone as hyperactive as Thatcher these were insufficient tasks to keep her busy, and since she had never developed a hinterland of outside interests, she soon returned to front-line British politics. She had supported Major's bid to succeed her, being determined to thwart Heseltine, and she was much relieved that he won the general election of April 1992, albeit with a much reduced majority. But though Thatcher would never feel the personal animosity towards Major that Heath continued to display towards her, she did not regard him as a figure of comparable stature to herself, and she was never fully reconciled to the fact that someone else had taken her place in 10 Downing Street. She regretted his attempts to embrace more consensual policies, as exemplified by his (very sensible) decision to replace the hated poll tax with a banded council tax. She felt vindicated in her long-standing opposition to the ERM when Britain was humiliatingly forced out of it in September 1992, and she deplored the Maastricht treaty, which Major had helped to negotiate, and which came into force in November 1993, because it greatly strengthened the central institutions of what had now become the European Union (EU), and also paved the way for the establishment of a single European currency. By means of such calculated and destructive interventions, Thatcher encouraged the Eurosceptics in the Tory party and the right-wing press, which undermined Major's authority and contributed to the landslide defeat at the general election of May 1997, a defeat which Thatcher (mistakenly) viewed as just punishment by the voters for his abandonment of her policies. Five years later she published *Statecraft: Strategies for a Changing World*, a coda to her memoirs, in which she once again denounced the EU.

Although she was increasingly becoming a caricature of her former self, Thatcher was much honoured in these later years. On becoming Tory leader, she had been made an honorary member of the hitherto all-male Carlton Club; eight years later she was (controversially) elected a fellow of the Royal Society; and in 1989 she was given the freedom of the City of London. Soon after her resignation as prime minister she had been made a member of the Order of Merit and Denis was given a baronetcy, and in 1991 she was awarded the Presidential Medal of Freedom by George H. W. Bush. The following year, having stood down from the Commons, she was created a life peer, and in 1995 she was appointed a lady of the Garter. From 1992 to 1998 she was chancellor of the University of Buckingham, and from 1993 to 2000 she was chancellor of the College of William and Mary in the United States. She unveiled a full-length statue of herself, intended for the central lobby of the Palace of Westminster, at the Guildhall Art Gallery in 1998, but it was decapitated by a protester in 2002 (it was subsequently restored and remains in its original location). Thatcher later unveiled another life-sized statue in the central lobby, the first occasion when a former prime minister had been commemorated in his or her lifetime. Every year the Falklands celebrate Margaret Thatcher day on 10 January, the date of her visit in 1983, but she remained conspicuously uncommemorated in Grantham at the time of her death.

Thatcher was often depicted in the media, and so was Denis. Throughout her time at 10 Downing Street, *Private Eye* ran a series of letters, purporting to be Denis's personal correspondence, but in fact written by Richard Ingrams and John Wells, which depicted him as a gin-swilling reactionary, with a keen eye for events and people, and always trying to escape the wrath of 'the Boss'. They gave rise to a number of annual editions of the collected 'Dear Bill' letters, and a stage version, *Anyone for Denis?*, was produced at the Whitehall Theatre in 1981, one performance of which the Thatchers gamely attended. Two years later the BBC commissioned Ian Curteis to write *The Falklands Play*, dramatizing the events of early 1982, and depicting Thatcher sympathetically as a strong leader. But the BBC refused to broadcast it while she was still in office, allegedly because it was too favourable to her, and it was not until 2002 that it was eventually produced on both radio and television. In 2004, BBC4 broadcast *The Long Walk to Finchley*, a drama based on Thatcher's early career; and in 2009 BBC2 produced *Margaret*, which focused on her fall from the premiership. Two years after, Meryl Streep played Thatcher in the film *The Iron Lady*. It met with mixed reviews, and was regarded by Thatcher's friends as in poor taste; but Streep's performance, for which she won an Oscar, was widely admired for its perfect rendition of Thatcher's voice and intonation, and for its vivid depiction of the dementia from which she was by then suffering.

Thatcher's last years were indeed sad and lonely. The earliest public indication of her physical and mental deterioration had been in 1994 when she lost consciousness at a speaking engagement in Chile. This was probably a minor stroke, and she began to experience short-term memory loss. She suffered another such incident in Madeira at the end of 2001, where she and Denis had returned to celebrate their golden wedding anniversary. Early the following year, after one more stroke, it was announced that she would undertake no more speaking engagements, although that did not prevent her attending Ronald Reagan's funeral in Washington in June 2004, or from delivering a pre-recorded tribute. By then Thatcher was truly alone, because exactly a year before, Denis had died of heart failure at the age of eighty-eight. For virtually the whole of their marriage, he had been her most loyal supporter, he had played the part of prime ministerial consort to perfection, and he was the best and perhaps the only real friend she ever had. In October 2005 Thatcher celebrated her eightieth birthday, at a party attended by the Queen, Prince Philip, and the prime minister, Tony Blair, and the following year she paid her last visit to the United States. In 2009 she fell and broke her arm; two years later her House of Lords office was closed; and in December 2012 she moved into a suite in the Ritz Hotel. There she died, following another stroke, on 8 April 2013, at the age of eighty-seven.

In death as in life Thatcher was controversial and divisive. The British newspapers that had supported her produced extended obituaries and lavish commemorative editions, and David Cameron and his prime ministerial predecessors paid fulsome tributes. But reactions were predictably more hostile in Argentina and South Africa; many Labour MPs boycotted a special Commons session devoted to applauding Thatcher's legacy; and there were spontaneous celebrations in former mining communities and in Glasgow, Brixton, Liverpool, Leeds, and Cardiff. The song 'Ding-Dong! The Witch is Dead' (from the musical *The Wizard of Oz*) rose to number two in the UK singles chart, there was an anti-Thatcher demonstration in Trafalgar Square, and there were fears that her ceremonial funeral might be marred by further protests; but in the event the crowds were generally peaceful. Planning for it had begun in 2009, under the appropriate codename of 'Operation True Blue', Thatcher had agreed all the details, and it was held in St Paul's Cathedral on 17 April 2013, in the presence of her friends and enemies from the British political establishment, and also the Queen and Prince Philip (who had not attended a former prime minister's funeral since Churchill's, in 1965). All living US presidents were invited: none attended (and nor did Gorbachev), but the American right was represented by Henry Kissinger, Dick Cheney, and Newt Gingrich, and former president de Klerk of South Africa was also among the mourners. After the service Thatcher's body was cremated, and her ashes were later interred in the grounds of the Royal Hospital, Chelsea, close by those of her husband.

Appraisal

Thatcher's magnificent obsequies invited comparison with those earlier accorded in the same church to Lord Nelson, the duke of Wellington, and Sir Winston Churchill. Did her life and achievements rank on the same epic scale as theirs? From one perspective, the answer must be no. The reconquest of the Falklands was an audacious military campaign, in which much bravery and great resourcefulness were displayed, not least by Thatcher herself, and which temporarily boosted national morale. But this late colonial expedition was not a victory to equal the battle of Trafalgar, the battle of Waterloo, or the battle of Britain, either in the scale of the conflict or, despite her claims to the contrary, in the world-historical significance of the outcome. However insistently and repeatedly she talked her country up, Thatcher's Britain possessed fewer ships than in Nelson's day, fewer troops than in Wellington's, and fewer fighter planes than in Churchill's, and this perforce limited what she could achieve on the global stage. But, from another perspective, these comparisons work to her advantage, for all three were born in circumstances and places more advantageous than hers: Nelson, the son of a clergyman, in a Norfolk rectory; Wellington, the younger son of an earl, in Dublin; and Churchill, the grandson of a duke, in Blenheim Palace. In making her life's journey from the Grantham grocer's shop to St Paul's Cathedral, Thatcher travelled further than they did, and had a much higher mountain to climb.

The more apt comparisons are with those other prime ministerial outsiders who, like Thatcher, started out with scarcely any advantages: Benjamin Disraeli, who was Jewish, a novelist, and chronically in debt in his early years; David Lloyd George, the son of a Welsh schoolteacher who died soon after he was born; Andrew Bonar Law, whose father was a clergyman in Canadian New Brunswick; Ramsay MacDonald, who was the illegitimate offspring of a farm labourer and born in Lossiemouth; James Callaghan, who was the son of a Royal Navy chief petty officer; and John Major, whose father was a music-hall performer who later made garden ornaments. Thatcher's social origins were inferior to Disraeli's, and closer to Lloyd George's and Bonar Law's, but they were superior to those of MacDonald, Callaghan, and Major. Moreover, and unlike any of them, Thatcher enjoyed two huge advantages: an Oxford education, which launched her into the élite social and political circles where she would spend the rest of her days, and a rich spouse who subordinated his life to hers. So, on balance, she was probably better placed by her twenties than they were, and she became an MP at an earlier age than any of them had been, except Disraeli and Bonar Law. In fact, the more appropriate resemblances are with Harold Wilson and Edward Heath (though neither would have been flattered by them). Like Thatcher, they were lowly born outside London, they went to grammar schools, and their lives were transformed, and their early disadvantages in great measure overcome, by their undergraduate years at Oxford.

But such comparisons are all with men, and as such they fail to do Thatcher justice, for it was as a woman in the overwhelmingly male world of politics that she was both uniquely disadvantaged, but also uniquely successful, and as prime minister for eleven years she set a record for continuity and endurance in the highest office that was unrivalled by any figure since Lord Liverpool. Throughout her premiership, she was *the* dominant figure in British public life, and she not only made the political weather, but went some way towards changing the political climate, too. At her best her energy was tireless, her stamina inexhaustible, her courage dauntless, and her patriotism beyond question. For much of her time as prime minister she commanded the cabinet, the civil service, the Commons, and parts of the country to a degree, and for a duration, which no other prime minister in modern times has rivalled. And on the international stage she possessed a star quality which no world leader in her day could equal, and which no twentieth-century British premier has attained, with the exception of Churchill. She was a force of nature, and for a time it did indeed seem as though she would go 'on and on and on and on'. The unrivalled ascendancy she achieved, and not only despite, but also because of, her gender, is vividly captured in a question which, well into her time at 10 Downing Street, a young boy put to his father: 'Daddy, are *men* ever prime minister in this country?'.

Such remarks could not be made about any other premier: as a woman of power there was no one in modern British history with whom Thatcher might be compared. But she was neither the first nor the only long-serving female prime minister in the second half of the twentieth century. Sirimavo Bandaranaike (Ceylon: 1960–65, 1970–79, and 1994–2000) got there well before her and lasted longer; Indira Gandhi (India: 1966–77 and 1980–84) was another precursor and contemporary; while Golda Meir (Israel, 1969–74), had come and gone before Thatcher arrived. During, and after, her time at 10 Downing Street there were two other women who held power for long spells: Gro Harlem Bruntland (Norway: 1981, 1986–9, and 1990–96), and Benazir

Bhutto (Pakistan: 1988–90 and 1993–6). From this global vantage point Thatcher appears less unique as a woman of power. Yet most of these comparisons also work to her advantage, for she made a greater international impact than any of them, and with one exception they all enjoyed an easier path into politics, and to the very top, than she did, thanks to the benefits of family connection and dynastic advantage. Mrs Bandaranaike took over as prime minister from her assassinated husband; Mrs Gandhi was Jawaharlal Nehru's daughter; Benazir Bhutto's father had been prime minister before her; and Gro Harlem Brundtland belonged to a prominent political family. Only Golda Meir came up by a route even harder than Thatcher's: for she, too, worked in the family's grocery shop, but did not marry a rich and supportive husband.

Thatcher's prime ministership combined a unique personal story with an extraordinary political dominance, and both were rendered the more remarkable on account of her gender. She also cared greatly about her posthumous reputation. But the verdicts of historians are neither uniform nor final, and least of all in the case of someone as controversial as she was—and still is. To her admirers she was the saviour of her country, who put the 'Great' back into Britain after decades of decline. Domestically she tamed the trades unions, reversed the trend towards nationalization, rolled back the state, created a vigorous enterprise economy, and forced the Labour Party to accept the brave new world she had created; while internationally she raised the Anglo-American relationship to levels of intimacy and importance not seen since the days of Churchill and Roosevelt, pioneered privatization which many other countries subsequently took up, and played a major part in ending the cold war and in bringing freedom and liberty to eastern Europe. But to her critics Thatcher was a narrow, provincial, and vindictive ideologue, whose hard-faced politics were devoid of compassion for the less well-off; increased inequality by legitimizing a culture of greed and by cutting taxes on the rich; undermined such bastions of liberal decency as the civil service, the universities, and the Church of England; destroyed the United Kingdom's sense of national solidarity and civic pride; and failed to invest the profits derived from North Sea oil and privatization in the country's long-term future.

These views are not easily reconciled, although there is some agreement that Thatcher performed better before 1986 than after, and also that she achieved less than she set out to do or claimed that she had done. Domestically she failed to curb public spending significantly; she did not change popular attitudes regarding the welfare state or the enterprise economy; and far from rolling back central government, she increased its intrusiveness and control in many areas of local and national life. As a global figure she was the first to recognize that the emergence of Gorbachev might lead to the ending of the cold war, but the unintended consequence was that Britain's influence in the United States and in Europe was diminished not enhanced, while in the case of German reunification and the collapse of apartheid in South Africa she was emphatically on the wrong side of history. She was also the beneficiary of deeper historical trends and longer-term changes which had nothing specific to do with her. The recession of the late 1970s and early 1980s was a global phenomenon, which resulted in a widespread turn to the right, not only in the United Kingdom but also in the United States, West Germany, Canada, Denmark, and Norway. In all these countries, the desire to reduce public spending, to balance the budget, to allow market forces free play, and to cut taxes became the stated aim of government policy (and the same was true of ostensibly left-wing administrations in Australia and New Zealand). And in Britain the shift from a northern-based industrial economy, with a manual, unionized working class, to a consumer-oriented, white-collar service economy increasingly concentrated in the south-east of England would have happened whoever might have occupied 10 Downing Street.

Yet the fact remains that Margaret Thatcher did more than anyone else to disrupt the political consensus that had existed from 1945 to 1979; she did shift the centre ground of public debate to the right; and after her fall in 1990, and even after her death in 2013, British politics on both the right and the left was largely played out in her shadow. All subsequent Tory leaders felt compelled to worship at Thatcher's shrine, even as they also sought, with varying degrees of conviction and success, to distance themselves from her and set new agendas. Lacking her prodigious energy, her global charisma, and her grassroots party support, none of them was as successful as she was in concealing the contradictions or in papering over the cracks of contemporary Conservatism: was it consensual or confrontational, compassionate or 'nasty', libertarian or controlling, populist or

authoritarian, English or British, pro- or anti-Europe, nationalistic or globalized? These questions remained unanswered. Meanwhile, under Tony Blair, New Labour's espousal of many Thatcherite nostrums paid enormous electoral dividends between 1997 and 2005, and Thatcher took all the credit she could for what seemed to be Labour's abandonment of socialism and nationalization, and its embrace of the free market, free enterprise and wealth creation; but after 2010 the party became increasingly uncomfortable with that accommodation and legacy, while the spectacular resurgence of Scottish nationalism owed at least as much to loathing of Thatcher as to the meltdown of Labour.

By her determined and assertive leadership Thatcher persuaded people, in Britain and elsewhere, that she was in command of events, and knew what to do and how to do it. She became the only twentieth-century premier to give her name to an ideology, but 'Thatcherism' was a political phenomenon rather than a coherent philosophy. She stressed her unswerving convictions and dislike of consensus, yet she could be more cautious and compromising than she admitted in public. She possessed some simple, core beliefs, but when it came to cutting public spending and income tax, to selling off nationalized industries, and to dealing with Europe, she often made things up as she went along. She stressed her integrity and preached the politics of morality, but she repeatedly resorted to devious means to undermine her cabinet colleagues. She relished battle and was a good cabinet 'butcher', devoid of sentiment or scruple, yet she was deeply hurt when she was finally paid out in her own coin. She abhorred class politics, but invariably championed the

lower and middle middle class, and she disliked the traditional working class, the public-school educated upper middle class, and most of the aristocracy. She was deeply and romantically patriotic, but this was not easily reconciled with her belief in free markets, liberal economics, and globalization. As Peregrine Worsthorne observed, she sought to make the world safe for the Victorian values of her father, yet she actually made it safer for the more suspect ethics of her son. 'You and I', she once told Bernard Ingham, 'are not *smooth* people'.[5] There are times when nations may need rough treatment. For good and for ill, Thatcher gave Britain plenty of it.

ENDNOTES

EPIGRAPH

1. Margaret Thatcher, *The Path to Power* (London: HarperCollins, 1995), p. 606

CHAPTER 1

1. ibid., p. 24
2. Charles Moore, *Margaret Thatcher: The Authorized Biography*, vol. 1, *Not For Turning* (London: Allen Lane, 2013), p. 30
3. P. Murray, *Margaret Thatcher: A Profile* (London: Star Books, 1978), p. 17
4. Hugo Young, *One of Us: A Biography of Margaret Thatcher* (London: Macmillan, 1989), p. 223
5. remarks outside 10 Downing Street, 4 May 1979, *Complete Public Statements*
6. speech at Lord Mayor's banquet, Mansion House, 15 Nov 1982, *Complete Public Statements*
7. Young, *One of Us*, p. 11
8. Hugo Young and Anne Sloman, *The Thatcher Phenomenon* (London: BBC, 1986), p. 17
9. ibid.

10. Charles Moore, *Margaret Thatcher: The Authorized Biography*, vol. 2, *Everything She Wants* (London: Allen Lane, 2015), p. 81
11. Thatcher, *The Path to Power*, p. 66

CHAPTER 2

1. *Evening Standard*, 15 October 1974
2. William Waldegrave, *A Different Kind of Weather* (London: Constable, 2015), p. 90
3. James Prior, *A Balance of Power* (London: Hamilton, 1986), p. 42
4. Thatcher, *The Path to Power*, p. 166
5. *The Sun*, 25 Nov 1971
6. Young, *One of Us*, p. 118
7. *The Independent*, 11 Sept 1999
8. *The Right Approach to the Economy* (London: Conservative and Unionist Central Office, 1977), p. 6

CHAPTER 3

1. speech to Conservative Central Council, Cardiff, 28 March 1981, *Complete Public Statements*
2. speech to Conservative Party Conference, 10 Oct 1980, *Complete Public Statements*
3. *The Times*, 30 March 1981
4. Jimmy Carter, *Keeping Faith: Memoirs of a President* (London: Collins, 1982), p. 113
5. speech to National Association of Evangelicals, Orlando, 8 March 1983, *Complete Public Statements*

CHAPTER 4

1. *The Times*, 15 Sept 1981
2. interview, Independent Radio News, 31 Dec 1981, *Complete Public Statements*
3. speech to Conservative rally at Cheltenham, 3 July 1982, *Complete Public Statements*
4. *New York Times*, 9 June 1982
5. speech to Conservative Party conference, 8 Oct 1982, *Complete Public Statements*
6. *Hansard*, House of Commons, fifth series, vol. 987, col. 742, 26 June 1980
7. Denis Healey, *The Time of My Life* (London: Michael Joseph, 1989), p. 500
8. *Daily Express*, 23 July 1982
9. BBC News, 28 Feb 1989

CHAPTER 5

1. Thatcher, *The Downing Street Years* (London: HarperCollins, 1993), p. 339
2. Moore, *Everything She Wants*, pp. 162, 167
3. Young, *One of Us*, p. 304
4. ibid, p. 306
5. *Woman's Own*, 31 Oct 1987
6. *Sunday Times*, 20 July 1986
7. Young, *One of Us*, p. 305
8. speech to National Union of Townswomen's Guilds Conference, 20 May 1965, *Complete Public Statements*
9. *Hansard*, House of Commons, fifth series, vol. 999, col. 447, 19 Feb 1981

10. Young, *One of Us*, p. 310
11. Dame Margery Corbett Ashby Memorial Lecture, 26 July 1982, *Complete Public Statements*
12. Moore, *Not for Turning*, p. 758
13. Young, *One of Us*, p. 383
14. speech to 1922 Committee, 19 July 1984, *Complete Public Statements*
15. *Hansard*, House of Commons, sixth series, vol. 90, col. 653, 27 Jan 1986

CHAPTER 6

1. speech to Conservative Central Council, 15 March 1986, *Complete Public Statements*
2. Carol Thatcher, *Below the Parapet: The Biography of Denis Thatcher* (London: HarperCollins, 1996), p. 246
3. speech to Conservative Central Council, 15 March 1986, *Complete Public Statements*
4. Nigel Lawson, *The View from No. 11: Memoirs of a Tory Radical* (London: Bantam Press, 1992), p. 573
5. Moore, *Everything She Wants*, p. 573
6. interview, BBC1, 17 Dec 1984, *Complete Public Statements*
7. Michael Dobbs, 'From Glory to Infamy', BBC Radio 4, 28 March 2010
8. John Campbell, *Margaret Thatcher*, vol. 2, *The Iron Lady* (London: Jonathan Cape, 2003), p. 537
9. interview for *Today* programme, BBC Radio 4, 6 June 1987, *Complete Public Statements*
10. press conference, 4 May 1989, *Complete Public Statements*
11. Campbell, *The Iron Lady*, p. 708

CHAPTER 7

1. speech at the Lord Mayor's banquet, Guildhall, 12 Nov 1990, *Complete Public Statements*
2. Thatcher, *The Downing Street Years*, p. 855
3. Young, *One of Us*, p. vii
4. speech to the College of Europe, 20 Sept 1988, *Complete Public Statements*
5. *Hansard*, House of Commons, sixth series, vol. 178, col. 873, 30 Oct 1990
6. *Hansard*, House of Commons, sixth series, vol. 180, col. 463 and col. 465, 13 Nov 1990

CHAPTER 8

1. Thatcher, *The Path to Power*, p. 465
2. R. Davenport-Hines and A. Sisman (eds), *One Hundred Letters from Hugh Trevor-Roper* (Oxford: Oxford University Press, 2014), p. 401
3. Margaret MacMillan, *History's People: Personalities and the Past* (Toronto: House of Anansi Press, 2015), p. 79
4. D. Palmer, *The Queen and Mrs Thatcher: An Inconvenient Relationship* (Stroud: The History Press, 2015), p. 201
5. Young, *One of Us*, p. 166

GUIDE TO FURTHER READING

Margaret Thatcher has been the most commented on, researched, and written about prime minister since Winston Churchill. Early books about her, as opposition leader and during her first years as premier, included both the adulatory – such as George Gardiner's study of *Margaret Thatcher: From Childhood to Leadership* (London: William Kimber, 1975), Ernle Money's *Margaret Thatcher: First Lady of the House* (London: Frewin, 1975), and Patricia Murray's *Margaret Thatcher: A Profile* (London: Star Books, 1978) – and the hostile, such as Stuart Hall and Martin Jacques's *The Politics of Thatcherism* (London: Lawrence and Wishart, 1983); Hall and Jacques had been among the first to identify 'Thatcherism' as a distinctive political creed, with the potential to re-orient British politics (in ways they did not like), in a series of seminal articles for the magazine *Marxism Today*. There was also considered contemporary analysis offered by seasoned journalists including Peter Riddell (*The Thatcher Government*, Oxford: M. Robertson, 1983, later followed by *The Thatcher Era and Its Legacy*, Oxford: Blackwell, 1991), Peter Jenkins (*Mrs Thatcher's Revolution*, London: Cape, 1987), and Hugo Young (*One of Us*, London: Macmillan,

1989), as well as early appraisals of Thatcher and her impact by political scientists including Dennis Kavanagh (*Thatcherism and British Politics*, Oxford: Oxford University Press, 1987), Andrew Gamble (*The Free Economy and the Strong State: The Politics of Thatcherism*, Durham, NC: Duke University Press, 1988), and the contributors to Robert Skidelsky's edited volume, *Thatcherism* (London: Chatto & Windus, 1989).

Even while Thatcher was still in Downing Street, the political battles of her premiership were being re-fought in the memoirs of her colleagues, as they would be in her own. The former began with Francis Pym's *The Politics of Consent* (London: Hamish Hamilton, 1984) and continued with autobiographies by James Prior (*A Balance of Power*, London: Hamish Hamilton, 1986), Michael Heseltine (*Where There's a Will*, London: Hutchinson, 1987), Norman Tebbit (*Upwardly Mobile*, London: Weidenfeld & Nicolson, 1988), and, after Thatcher's resignation, Bernard Ingham (*Kill the Messenger*, London: HarperCollins, 1991), Nigel Lawson (*The View from No. 11: Memoirs of a Tory Radical*, London: Bantam Press, 1992), and Geoffrey Howe (*Conflict of Loyalty*, London: Macmillan, 1994), among many others. Thatcher's own memoirs appeared in two volumes with Rupert Murdoch's Harper Collins: *The Downing Street Years* (1993), covering her premiership, and *The Path to Power* (1995), dealing with her earlier life. These and other belligerent and partisan retrospections were deftly finessed by John Campbell in his biography, *Margaret Thatcher*, Vol. 1, *The Grocer's Daughter*, and Vol. 2, *The Iron Lady* (London: Jonathan Cape, 2000 and 2003).

Thatcher's retirement from public life, along with the opening up of her own vast archive as well as the public records, initiated a new phase of academic research. In 1998 Oxford University Press published a fully searchable CD-ROM edited by Chris Collins, *Margaret Thatcher: The Complete Public Statements*, which enabled the user to browse and research her public utterances ranging from radio interviews to answers to prime minister's questions; much of the content of this disk has now been put online, along with other public papers and a range of helpful contextual material, by the Margaret Thatcher Foundation at http://www.margaretthatcher.org/. Simultaneously, the Policy Institute at King's College London has been publishing online the results of an oral history project on 'Margaret Thatcher and No. 10', at http://www.thatcherandnumberten.com/. Thatcher's own vast archive, comprising more than one million documents and occupying some three hundred metres of shelving, has been deposited at the Churchill Archives Centre in Cambridge (pointedly not in her *alma mater*'s Bodleian Library), and is gradually being opened up to researchers. Among the other items there is the handbag which she famously swung at cabinet meetings and international summits in the mid-1980s.

The wealth of new material on Thatcher, and her prominence in British politics, have given rise to a veritable academic industry, with many hundreds of journal articles and dozens of books already exploring one aspect or another of her ideas, aims, policies, or image. A particularly useful collection of assessments was published as a special issue of the journal *British Politics* in April 2015, as '25 Years On . . . The Legacy of Thatcher and Thatcherism'. Much of this academic research on Thatcher, as well as the vast written and spoken legacy of

Thatcher herself, has been incorporated into the official biography by Charles Moore, *Margaret Thatcher*, Vol. 1, *Not For Turning*, and Vol. 2, *Everything She Wants* (London: Allen Lane, 2013 and 2015), and its impending completion in a third volume will signal the end of another phase of interpretation and historiography. It seems clear that Margaret Thatcher will continue to fascinate biographers and historians for many years to come; but already, a more nuanced and complex picture has emerged of someone who, in her public images and political utterances, made certainty and confrontation her stock-in-trade.

DRAMATIS PERSONAE

Armstrong, Robert, Baron Armstrong of Ilminster (b. 1927) Civil servant; permanent secretary, Home Office, 1977–9; cabinet secretary, 1979–87, and head of the home civil service, 1983–7; kt 1978, life peer 1988

Baker, Kenneth, Baron Baker of Dorking (b. 1934) Conservative politician; MP 1968–70 and 1970–97; junior minister, Trade and Industry (1981–4), Environment (1984–5); secretary of state for Environment, 1985–6, Education and Science, 1986–90; chancellor of Duchy of Lancaster and Conservative party chairman, 1989–90; Home secretary, 1990–2; life peer 1997

Benn, Tony, formerly Anthony Wedgwood Benn; briefly 2nd Viscount Stansgate (1925–2014) Labour politician; MP 1956–60, 1963–83 and 1984–2001; postmaster-general, 1964–6; Minister of Technology, 1966–70; secretary of state for Industry, 1974–5, Energy, 1975–9; leading figure on Labour left; succeeded father 1960 but renounced peerage 1963

Bowyer, Sir Eric (1902–1964) Civil servant; permanent secretary, Ministry of Materials, 1953–4, Ministry of Pensions and National Insurance, 1955–64; kt 1950

Brittan, Leon, Baron Brittan of Spennithorne (1939–2015) Conservative politician; MP 1974–88; junior minister, Home Office, 1979–81, Treasury, 1981–3; Home secretary, 1983–5; secretary of state for Trade and Industry, 1985–6; member, European Commission, 1989–99; kt 1989, life peer 2000

Bush, George H.W. (b. 1924) Oil executive, US Republican politician; congressman, 1967–71; vice-president of USA, 1981–9; president of USA, 1989–93

Butler, Robin, Baron Butler of Brockwell (b. 1938) Civil servant; principal private secretary to prime minister, 1982–5; second permanent secretary, Treasury, 1985–7; cabinet secretary and head of home civil service, 1988–98; kt 1988, life peer 1998

Callaghan, James (Jim), Baron Callaghan of Cardiff (1912–2005) Labour politician; MP 1945–87; chancellor of the exchequer, 1964–7; Home secretary, 1967–70; Foreign secretary, 1974–6; prime minister, 1976–9; leader of opposition, 1979–80; life peer 1987

Carrington, Peter, 6th Baron Carrington (b. 1919) Conservative politician; succeeded father 1938; junior minister, 1951–6; first lord of Admiralty, 1959–63; leader of House of Lords, 1963–4; secretary of state for Defence, 1970–4, Energy, 1974; Foreign secretary, 1979–82

Carter, James (Jimmy) (b. 1924) Peanut farmer, US Democrat politician; congressman, 1963–7; governor of Georgia, 1971–5; president of USA, 1977–81

Castle, Barbara, Baroness Castle of Blackburn (1910–2002) Labour politician; MP 1945–79; minister of Overseas Development, 1964–5, Transport, 1965–8; secretary of state for Employment, 1968–70, Social Services, 1974–6; MEP 1979–89; life peer 1990

Clark, Alan (1928–1999) Conservative politician; MP 1974–92 and 1997–9; junior minister, Employment, 1983–6, Trade, 1986–9, Defence, 1989–92; best known for publication of *Diaries*

Clarke, Kenneth (Ken) (b. 1940) Conservative politician; MP since 1970; government whip, 1972–4; junior minister, Transport, 1979–82, Health and Social Security, 1982–5; paymaster general, 1985–7; chancellor of Duchy of Lancaster, 1987–8; secretary of state for Health, 1988–90, Education and Science, 1990–2; Home secretary, 1992–3; chancellor of the exchequer, 1993–7; lord chancellor, 2010–12; minister without portfolio, 2012–14

Delors, Jacques (b. 1925) French socialist politician; minister of finance, 1981–4; president of European Commission, 1985–95

Foot, Michael (1913–2010) Labour politician; MP 1945–55 and 1960–92; secretary of state for Employment, 1974–6; leader of House of Commons, 1976–9; leader of opposition, 1980–3

Galtieri, Leopoldo (1926–2003) Argentine general and dictator; career army officer; commander in chief, 1980; unelected president of Argentina, 1981–2; imprisoned for incompetence 1986–90; under house arrest for human rights abuses 2002

Gilmour, Ian, Baron Gilmour of Craigmillar (1926–2007) Conservative politician; MP 1962–92; junior minister, Defence, 1970–4, secretary of state for Defence, 1974; lord privy seal, 1979–81; succeeded father as baronet 1977, life peer 1992

Gorbachev, Mikhail (b. 1931) Russian politician; last general secretary of Communist Party of Soviet Union, 1985–93; last president of Soviet Union, 1990–1; introduced *glasnost* ('openness') and *perestroika* ('reform'), leading to end of Soviet communism

Gow, Ian (1937–1990) Conservative politician; MP 1974–90; parliamentary private secretary to prime minister, 1979–83; junior minister, Housing and Construction, 1983–5, Treasury, 1985; murdered by IRA

Harris, Ralph, Baron Harris of High Cross (1924–2006) Economist and political thinker; founding director, 1957–87, chairman, 1987–9, joint president, 1990 onwards, Institute of Economic Affairs; life peer 1979

Hayek, Friedrich August (1899–1992) Austrian-born economist; British subject, 1938; later based in USA and Germany; leading figure in revival of liberal economics and rise of monetarism; Nobel prize 1974

Heath, Sir Edward (1916–2005) Conservative politician; MP 1950–2001; junior whip, 1951–5, chief whip, 1955–9; minister of Labour, 1959–60; lord privy seal, 1960–3; secretary of state for

Industry and Trade, 1963–4; leader of opposition, 1965–70; prime minister, 1970–4; leader of opposition, 1974–5; kt 1992

Heseltine, Michael, Baron Heseltine (b. 1933) Publisher, Conservative politician; MP 1966–2001; junior minister, Transport, 1970, Environment, 1970–2, Trade and Industry, 1972–4; secretary of state for Environment, 1979–83, Defence, 1983–6; secretary of state for Environment, 1990–2, Trade, 1992–5; deputy prime minister, 1995–7; life peer 2001

Hogg, Quintin, Baron Hailsham of St Marylebone (1907–2001) Lawyer, Conservative politician; MP 1938–50 and 1963–70; junior minister, Air, 1945; first lord of the Admiralty, 1956–7; minister of Education, 1957; lord president of the council, 1957–9 and 1960–4; lord privy seal, 1959–60; secretary of state for Education, 1964; lord high chancellor, 1970–4 and 1979–87; succeeded father as 2nd Viscount Hailsham 1950, disclaimed peerages 1963, life peer 1970

Home, Alexander (Alec) Douglas-, Baron Home of the Hirsel (1903–1995) Conservative politician; MP 1931–51 and 1963–74; junior minister, Foreign Office, 1945, Scottish Office, 1951–5; Commonwealth secretary, 1955–60, Foreign secretary, 1960–3; prime minister, 1963–4; leader of opposition, 1964–5; Foreign secretary, 1970–4; succeeded father as 14th Earl of Home 1951, disclaimed peerages 1963, kt 1962, life peer 1974

Howe, Geoffrey, Baron Howe of Aberavon (1926–2015) Barrister, Conservative politician; MP 1964–92; solicitor-general, 1970–2; junior minister, Trade and Industry, 1972–4; chancellor of the exchequer, 1979–83; Foreign secretary, 1983–9; lord president of the council and deputy prime minister, 1989–90; kt 1970, life peer 1992

Hurd, Douglas, Baron Hurd of Westwell (b. 1930) Diplomat, Conservative politician; MP 1974–97; junior minister, Foreign Office, 1979–83, Home Office, 1983–4; secretary of state for Northern Ireland, 1984–5; Home secretary, 1985–9; Foreign secretary, 1989–95; life peer 1997

Ingham, Sir Bernard (b. 1932) Journalist and press officer; entered journalism 1948; director of information, Employment, 1973, Energy, 1974–7; civil servant, Energy, 1978–9; chief press secretary to prime minister, 1979–90; kt 1990

Jenkins, Roy, Baron Jenkins of Hillhead (1920–2003) Labour, Social Democrat and Liberal Democrat politician; MP 1948–76, 1982–7; junior minister, Commonwealth, 1949–50; minister of Aviation, 1964–5; Home secretary, 1965–7 and 1974–6; chancellor of the exchequer, 1967–70; president, European Commission, 1977–81; co-founder, Social Democratic Party, 1981; life peer 1987

Joseph, Keith, Baron Joseph (1918–1994) Barrister, Conservative politician; MP 1956–87; junior minister, Commonwealth, 1957–9, Housing, 1959–61, Trade, 1961–2; minister of Housing, 1962–4; secretary of state for Social Services, 1970–4, Industry, 1979–81, Education and Science, 1981–6; succeeded father as baronet 1944, life peer 1987

Kinnock, Neil, Baron Kinnock (b. 1942) Labour politician; MP 1970–95; junior minister, Employment, 1974–5; leader of opposition, 1983–92; member of European Commission, 1995–2004; life peer 2005

Kohl, Helmut (b. 1930) German Christian Democrat politician; minister-president of Rhineland-Palatinate, 1969–76; chairman of Christian Democratic Union, 1973–98; chancellor of Germany, 1982–98; oversaw reunification of Germany, 1990

Lawson, Nigel, Baron Lawson of Blaby (b. 1932) Financial journalist, Conservative politician; MP 1974–92; financial secretary to Treasury, 1979–81; secretary of state for Energy, 1981–3; chancellor of the exchequer, 1983–9; life peer 1992

Macmillan, Harold, 1st Earl of Stockton (1894–1986) Conservative politician; MP 1924–9, 1931–45, 1945–64; junior minister, Supply, 1940–2, Colonies, 1942; minister resident, north-west Africa, 1942–5, Air secretary, 1945; minister of Housing, 1951–4, Defence, 1954–5; Foreign secretary, 1955; chancellor of the exchequer, 1955–7; prime minister, 1957–63; created earl 1984

Major, Sir John (b. 1943) Banker, Conservative politician; MP 1979–2001; junior minister, Home Office, 1981–3; junior whip, 1983–5; junior minister, Health and Social Security, 1985–7; chief secretary to Treasury, 1987–9; Foreign secretary, 1989; chancellor of the exchequer, 1989–90; prime minister, 1990–7; kt 2005

Mandela, Nelson (1918–2013) South African politician; leading figure in African National Congress; imprisoned, 1962–90; first president of post-*apartheid* South Africa, 1994–9

Maudling, Reginald (1917–1979) Conservative politician; MP 1950–79; junior minister, Civil Aviation, 1952, Treasury, 1952–5; minister of Supply, 1955–7; paymaster-general, 1957–9; Trade secretary, 1959–61; secretary of state for Colonies, 1961–2; chancellor of the exchequer, 1962–4; Home secretary, 1970–2

Mitterrand, François (1916–1996) French socialist politician; minister for Veterans, 1947–8, Overseas France, 1950–1, Interior, 1954–5, Justice, 1956–7; first secretary of Socialist Party, 1971–81; president of France, 1981–95

Murdoch, Rupert (b. 1931) Australian-born media magnate; American citizen, 1985; extensive media interests, especially in Australia, USA, UK; chairman and chief executive, News Corporation; owned, among others, *Sun*, *News of the World*, *Times*, *Sunday Times*, and controlling stake in Sky satellite television in UK

Neave, Airey (1916–1979) Conservative politician; MP 1953–79; junior minister, Transport, 1954, Colonies, 1954–6, Transport, 1957–9, Air, 1959; organized Thatcher's campaign for leadership, 1975; head of Thatcher's private office and spokesman on Northern Ireland, 1975–9; murdered by Irish National Liberation Army

Nott, Sir John (b. 1932) Conservative politician; MP 1966–83; junior minister, Treasury, 1972–4; secretary of state for Trade, 1979–81, Defence, 1981–3; kt 1983

Parkinson, Cecil, Baron Parkinson (1931–2016) Conservative politician; MP 1970–92; junior minister, Trade and Industry, 1972–4, Trade, 1979–81; paymaster general, 1981–3; secretary of state for Trade and Industry, 1983, Energy, 1987–9, Transport, 1989–90; life peer 1992

Pile, Sir William (1919–1997) Civil servant; permanent secretary, Education and Science, 1970–6; chairman, Board of Inland Revenue, 1976–9; kt 1971

Powell, Charles, Baron Powell of Bayswater (b. 1941) Career diplomat; counsellor for Rhodesia negotiations, 1979–80; private secretary to prime minister, 1983–91; kt 1990, life peer 2000

Prior, James (Jim), Baron Prior (b. 1927) Conservative politician; MP 1959–87; junior minister, Trade, 1963, Power, 1963–4; minister of Agriculture, 1970–2; leader of House of Commons, 1972–4; secretary of state for Employment, 1979–81, Northern Ireland, 1981–4; life peer 1987

Pym, Francis, Baron Pym (1922–2008) Conservative politician; MP 1961–87; junior whip, 1962–4; chief whip, 1970–3; secretary of state for Northern Ireland, 1973–4, Defence, 1979–81; leader of House of Commons, 1981–2; Foreign secretary, 1982–3; life peer 1987

Reagan, Ronald (1911–2004) Actor, US Republican politician; governor of California, 1967–75; president of USA, 1981–9

Reece, Sir Gordon (1929–2001) Journalist, television producer, public affairs consultant; ITV from 1960; adviser to Margaret Thatcher, 1975–9; director of publicity, Conservative Central Office, 1978–80; kt 1986

Ridley, Nicholas, Baron Ridley of Liddlesdale (1929–1993) Conservative politician; MP 1959–92; junior minister, Education, 1962–4, Technology, 1970, Trade and Industry, 1970–2, Foreign Office, 1979–81, Treasury, 1981–3; secretary of state for Transport, 1983–6, Environment, 1986–9, Trade and Industry, 1989–90; life peer 1992

Roberts, Alfred (1892–1970) Margaret's father; grocer; JP; mayor of Grantham 1945–6

Roberts, Beatrice (née Stephenson) (1888–1960) Margaret's mother

Roberts, Muriel (married name Cullen) (1921–2004) Margaret's sister; physiotherapist

Scargill, Arthur (b. 1938) Trade unionist; miner, 1953; NUM branch committee, 1960, national executive, 1972; president, NUM, 1981–2002; co-founder, Socialist Labour Party, 1996

Seldon, Arthur (1916–2005) Economist; editorial director, Institute of Economic Affairs, 1957–88; founding editor, *Economic Affairs*, 1980; joint president, Institute of Economic Affairs, 1990 on

Soames, Christopher, Baron Soames (1920–1987) Conservative politician, son-in-law of Winston Churchill; MP 1950–66; junior minister, Air, 1955–7, Admiralty, 1957–8; secretary of state for War, 1958–60, minister of Agriculture, 1960–4; ambassador to France, 1968–72; member of European Commission, 1973–7; kt 1973, life peer 1978; governor of Southern Rhodesia, 1979–80; leader of House of Lords, 1979–81

Tebbit, Norman, Baron Tebbit (b. 1931) Conservative politician; MP 1970–92; junior minister, Employment, 1972–3, Trade, 1979–81, Industry, 1981; secretary of state for Employment, 1981–3, Trade and Industry, 1983–5; chairman, Conservative Party, 1985–7; life peer 1992

Thatcher, Carol (b. 1953) Margaret's daughter; freelance journalist and media personality; author of several books including biography of father

Thatcher, Sir Denis (1915–2003) Margaret's husband; businessman (Atlas Preservative, Castrol, Burmah Oil); golfer; created baronet 1991

Thatcher, Sir Mark (b. 1953) Margaret's son; businessman (motor racing, construction, property, loans, arms); prosecuted for tax evasion in US, 1996, moved to South Africa; convicted in South Africa, 2005, for role in Equatorial Guinea coup attempt; succeeded father 2003

Waldegrave, William, Baron Waldegrave of North Hill (b. 1946) Conservative politician; MP 1979–97; junior minister,

Education and Science, 1981–3, Environment, 1983–8, Foreign Office, 1988–90; secretary of state for Health, 1990–2; chancellor of Duchy of Lancaster, 1992–4; minister of Agriculture, 1994–5; chief secretary to Treasury, 1995–7; life peer 1999

Walters, Sir Alan (1926–2009) economist; academic appointments at Birmingham, 1951–68, LSE, 1968–76, Johns Hopkins, 1976–91; adviser to World Bank, 1976–80 and 1984–8, prime minister, 1981–4 and 1989; kt 1983

Whitelaw, William, 1st Viscount Whitelaw (1918–1999) farmer, Conservative politician; MP 1955–83; junior minister, Trade, 1956, Treasury, 1957–8; junior whip, 1959–62; junior minister, Labour, 1962–4; leader of House of Commons, 1970–2; secretary of state for Northern Ireland, 1972–3, Employment, 1973–4; Home secretary, 1979–83; created viscount 1983; leader of House of Lords, 1983–8

Wilson, Harold, Baron Wilson of Rievaulx (1916–1995) Economist, Labour politician; MP 1945–83; junior minister, Works, 1945–7, Overseas Trade, 1947; Trade secretary, 1947–51; leader of opposition, 1963–4 and 1970–4; prime minister, 1964–70 and 1974–6; life peer 1983

GLOSSARY

African National Congress (ANC) The main opposition grouping fighting the apartheid regime in South Africa, and the governing party in South Africa after the first democratic elections in 1994

Anglo-Irish Agreement Signed by Thatcher and Garrett FitzGerald on 15 November 1985 guaranteeing no change in Northern Ireland's constitutional position without majority consent, but giving the Republic of Ireland an advisory role in the governance of Northern Ireland

apartheid 'Separateness'; the policy of strict racial segregation enforced by the ruling National Party in South Africa from 1948 to 1994

'Big Bang' The deregulation of the securities market in the City of London on 27 October 1986, when the London Stock Exchange became a private limited company

cabinet The senior 20–24 politicians in the governing party or coalition who in theory collectively form the highest level of government (the prime minister being 'first among equals'), and all but a handful of whom have individual responsibility for a government department

Campaign for Nuclear Disarmament (CND) Movement founded in 1957 to advocate unilateral nuclear disarmament by the UK as a step to global disarmament; peaked in early 1980s

Centre for Policy Studies Think-tank founded by Sir Keith Joseph and others in 1974 to champion classical liberal economics; early advocates of monetarism, deregulation, privatization

closed shop A practice whereby employment in a certain trade or company either was restricted to members of a given trade union or carried with it an obligation to join a trade union

Common Market The UK term for the European Economic Community, one of the three European Communities (see below)

community charge Otherwise known as 'poll tax'; the form of local taxation introduced in Scotland in 1989 and in England and Wales in 1990, replacing a property tax (rates) by a uniform individual tax

comprehensive schooling A system of public-funded schools which have no selection criteria

European Communities The European Economic Community (otherwise known as the Common Market), the European Atomic Energy Community, and the European Coal and Steel Community, which the UK joined in 1973; merged as one of three 'pillars' of the European Union in 1993

Exchange Rate Mechanism (ERM) Established 1979, a precursor to the euro, which sought to reduce exchange rate instability by tying European currencies within margins of each other; UK a member 1990–2

Greater London Council (GLC) London-wide administrative body in existence from 1965 to 1986; abolished by Thatcher, and powers largely devolved to boroughs before formation of the Greater London Authority in 2000

Institute for Economic Affairs Think-tank founded by Antony Fisher in 1955 to promote classical liberal economics and free market ideas

Irish Republican Army (IRA) Usually refers to the Provisional IRA, formed in 1969 in a split from the Official IRA; pursued violent action to further the aim of a reunification of Ireland; agreed to ceasefire in 1997

junior minister A member of the government who serves in the second tier, not part of the cabinet, and usually directly under a cabinet minister

Keynesianism A set of economic theories associated with or derived from John Maynard Keynes, which among other things validate an interventionist role for the government in the economy, particularly during recessions

Methodism An offshoot of the Church of England based on the teachings of John Wesley (1703–1791), with an emphasis on the primacy of scripture and good works

monetarism An economic theory that tight control of the money supply restrains inflation and promotes economic growth

Open University Distance learning and research university established in 1969, first students enrolled in 1971

poll tax See community charge

prices and incomes policy A tool of state intervention in economic management aimed at by both Labour and Conservative governments before Thatcher, to restrain inflation by means of statutory control of wages and prices; introduced by Heath in 1972

privatization The return to the private sector of previously nationalized (or government-owned and -run) industries

Single European Act Treaty signed by EC member states in February 1986 (in two cohorts: Thatcher signed on behalf of the UK on 17 February), establishing a timetable for creating a single market and introducing qualified majority voting in the Council of Ministers (representing governments) to achieve it

stagflation A combination of economic stagnation and inflation (difficult to explain through conventional Keynesian economics)

Thatcherism A set of beliefs, attitudes and policies variously defined, but with at its core a belief in free market economics and a 'small state'

Tory Conservative

Unilateral Declaration of Independence (UDI) A declaration on 11 November 1965 by the white minority regime in

Southern Rhodesia that it regarded itself as fully independent of the UK; 'rebellion' ended with return to colonial rule in 1979 and independence in 1980 as Zimbabwe

Westland affair Cabinet crisis in 1985–6; began as a dispute over rival US and European bids for Westland Helicopters, but focused on issues of integrity, including the leaking of private correspondence

'wets' Centrist or 'one nation' Conservatives, more inclined to government economic intervention and more extensive welfare provision than 'Thatcherites'

whip A party political post in the House of Commons and House of Lords whose incumbent is responsible for trying to ensure party discipline

CHRONOLOGY

13 Oct 1925	born in Grantham
Sept 1936	begins education at Kesteven and Grantham Girls' School
Oct 1943	begins chemistry degree at Somerville College, Oxford
Oct 1946	elected President of Oxford University Conservative Association
June 1947	completes chemistry degree
31 Jan 1949	selected as Conservative candidate for Dartford
23 Feb 1950	general election: defeated at Dartford, Labour government formed
25 Oct 1951	general election: defeated at Dartford, Conservative government formed
13 Dec 1951	marriage to Denis Thatcher
Jan 1952	begins legal training; resigns as candidate for Dartford
15 Aug 1953	birth of Carol and Mark Thatcher
1 Dec 1953	qualifies as a barrister
31 July 1958	adopted as Conservative candidate for Finchley
8 Oct 1959	general election: elected MP for Finchley, Conservative government formed
5 Feb 1960	makes maiden speech in House of Commons

9 Oct 1961	appointed parliamentary under-secretary for Pensions and National Insurance
10 Oct 1963	Harold Macmillan resigns as prime minister, succeeded by Alec Douglas-Home
15 Oct 1964	general election: Labour government formed, Thatcher shadows pensions
25 July 1965	Douglas-Home resigns as Conservative leader, succeeded by Edward Heath
18 Oct 1965	moves to shadow Housing and Land
31 March 1966	general election: Labour remain in power
19 April 1966	moves to shadow Treasury as deputy to Iain Macleod
10 Oct 1967	appointed to shadow cabinet, responsible for Fuel and Power
14 Nov 1968	moves to shadow Transport
21 Oct 1969	moves to shadow Education
18 June 1970	general election: Conservative government formed, Thatcher becomes secretary of state for Education and Science
30 June 1970	issues Circular 10/70, withdrawing compulsory move to comprehensive schooling
6 Dec 1972	publishes white paper, *Education: A Framework for Expansion*
28 Feb 1974	general election: minority Labour government formed, Thatcher shadows Environment
10 Oct 1974	general election: Labour government formed with slim majority
7 Nov 1974	Thatcher moves to shadow Treasury as deputy to Robert Carr
21 Nov 1974	decides to run for leadership of Conservative Party
4 Feb 1975	defeats Heath in first ballot for Conservative leadership; Heath resigns

11 Feb 1975	elected Conservative leader on second ballot
5 April 1976	James Callaghan elected Labour leader, becomes prime minister
3 May 1979	general election: Conservative government formed with majority of 43, Thatcher becomes prime minister
25 Dec 1979	Russia invades Afghanistan
18 April 1980	Zimbabwe becomes independent
26 March 1981	Social Democratic Party formed
30 March 1981	364 economists write to *Times* to denounce Thatcher's economic policies
2 April 1982	Argentina invades Falklands
14 June 1982	Falklands: Argentine surrender
9 June 1983	general election: Conservative government increases majority to 144
25 Nov 1983	US invasion of Grenada
12 March 1984	miners' strike begins
25-26 June 1984	Fontainebleau European Council: British rebate on European budget
12 Oct 1984	Brighton bombing (IRA attempt to assassinate Thatcher)
16 Dec 1984	Mikhail Gorbachev visits Chequers
19 Dec 1984	Thatcher signs Joint Agreement with China on Hong Kong
3 March 1985	end of miners' strike
15 Nov 1985	Anglo-Irish Agreement
2 Dec 1985	Luxembourg European Council: Single European Act agreed
9 Jan 1986	Michael Heseltine resigns over Westland affair
11 June 1987	general election: Conservative government re-elected with majority of 102
26 Oct 1989	Nigel Lawson resigns as chancellor of the exchequer

31 March 1990	'poll tax' riot in Trafalgar Square
2 Aug 1990	Iraq invades Kuwait
3 Oct 1990	German reunification
5 Oct 1990	UK joins Exchange Rate Mechanism
1 Nov 1990	Geoffrey Howe resigns
14 Nov 1990	Heseltine stands for Conservative leadership
20 Nov 1990	Conservative leadership election first ballot
22 Nov 1990	Thatcher announces decision not to contest second ballot
28 Nov 1990	resigns as prime minister, succeeded by John Major
30 June 1992	enters House of Lords as Baroness Thatcher
26 June 2003	Denis Thatcher dies
8 April 2013	Margaret Thatcher dies
17 April 2013	funeral at St Paul's Cathedral

OPINION POLLS

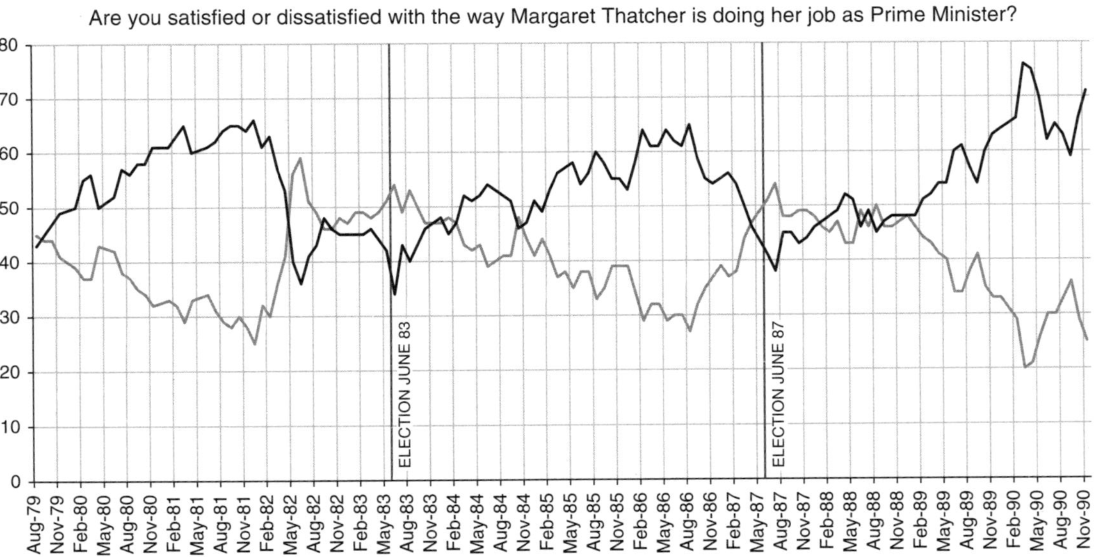
Are you satisfied or dissatisfied with the way Margaret Thatcher is doing her job as Prime Minister?
80
70
60
50
40
30
20
10
0
Aug-79
Nov-79
Feb-80
May-80
Aug-80
Nov-80
Feb-81
May-81
Aug-81
Nov-81
Feb-82
May-82
Aug-82
Nov-82
Feb-83
May-83
Aug-83
Nov-83
Feb-84
May-84
Aug-84
Nov-84
Feb-85
May-85
Aug-85
Nov-85
Feb-86
May-86
Aug-86
Nov-86
Feb-87
May-87
Aug-87
Nov-87
Feb-88
May-88
Aug-88
Nov-88
Feb-89
May-89
Aug-89
Nov-89
Feb-90
May-90
Aug-90
Nov-90
ELECTION JUNE 83
ELECTION JUNE 87
Percentage Satisfied
Percentage Dissatisfied
© Ipsos Mori. Used with permission.

INDEX